Exploring Your Identity, Sharpening Your Focus

Tim Elmore

foreword by John Maxwell

© Copyright 2011 Tim Elmore
All rights reserved.

No part of this work may be reproduced or transmitted in any form or by any means, electronic or mechanical, including photocopying and recording, or by any information storage or retrieval system, except as may be expressly permitted in writing by the publisher. Requests for permission should be sent in writing to Growing Leaders, 270 Scientific Drive, Suite 10, Norcross, GA 30092

ISBN: 0-6330-9862-0

Dewey Decimal Classification Number: 248.834
Subject Heading: STUDENTS/LIFE CALLING/LEADERSHIP
Printed in the United States of America

Unless otherwise indicated, all Scripture quotations are taken from the New International Version (NIV) Bible® Copyright © 1999, 2000, 2002, 2003. Used by permission.

Scripture taken from THE MESSAGE. Copyright © by Eugene H. Peterson, 1993, 1994, 1995. Used by permission of NavPress Publishing Group.

Cover Illustration: Jeff Gribble / www.DesignIndustry.com

CONTENTS

Foreword by John Maxwell

5   **SESSION 1**
The Life You Were Meant to Live

25   **SESSION 2**
Deepening Your Intimacy with God

41   **SESSION 3**
Who Do You Think You Are?

57   **SESSION 4**
Exercising Spiritual Disciplines

73   **SESSION 5**
Playing to Your Strengths

89   **SESSION 6**
The Heart of a Servant

105   **SESSION 7**
Building Healthy Emotions

121   **SESSION 8**
The Power of Passion

FOREWORD

I have said for many years that leadership is influence. It isn't about positions or titles or badges. I like how my colleague Tim Elmore describes it: it is about leveraging your God-given influence for a worthwhile cause.

Throughout my career, I have had countless people ask me these two questions: "Isn't leadership a gift? If so, how can you encourage everyone to be a leader?"

My answer is yes—leadership is a gift. It is a spiritual gift listed in Romans 12. For others, it is a God-given talent. Some people just seem to be natural leaders. I believe these kind of people need to find places to lead and use their gift. However, just because leadership is a gift doesn't mean everyone else is called to merely follow. Everyone leads and influences people. Some are gifted to influence others, but all of us should use our influence for the Kingdom of God. It works just like evangelism. Some people have this gift (Ephesians 4:10-11) and naturally share their faith with others. However, all of us are called to be a witness for Christ. So, the answer is the same to both of these questions:

- Is leadership a spiritual gift? Yes.
- Is everyone called to lead in some way? Yes.

This book is about helping you live a life of influence, even after you leave the comfortable "bubble" at your school. It is a book for anyone—but it is especially directed at young leaders who are entering the marketplace and want to continue making a difference in the lives of the people around them. It will enable you to live out your purpose and passions and influence the world by doing so. It is a deeply reflective book, challenging you to sort out your life mission, your values, your network of relationships, your identity, your emotional security and your calling to serve in the area of your strengths. I highly recommend you work through this book with an accountability partner, a small group or a mentoring community. Interact over the principles; pray for one another and apply them as you learn them.

Tim Elmore has worked with me since 1983. We have had a Paul and Timothy relationship, and Tim has always been a "next generation leader." He has worked with students for more than thirty years, and I don't know anyone who can communicate leadership truths better than Tim. I love his emphasis on the heart. You must prepare your heart before you prepare your hands to lead. The vast majority of your influence doesn't spring from outward techniques or mechanics. It will come from the invisible qualities inside of you. May this book guide you through some "heart surgery."

If you like what you receive here, check out other ideas and resources Tim has available from "Growing Leaders" at: www.GrowingLeaders.com.

May this book prepare you for a lifetime of influence. May you be "salt" and "light" in your world for years to come.

Dr. John C. Maxwell
Best selling author
Founder, The John Maxwell Company

THE LIFE YOU WERE MEANT TO LIVE

Embracing Your God-Given Mission in Life Will Give You Direction

*"I have glorified You on the earth by
completing the work You gave Me to do."*
— Jesus Christ (John 17:4)

LINKING YOUR LIFE TO GOD'S PURPOSE FOR THE WORLD
The study guide you're about to experience was created to help you go deeper, as you seek to live your life on purpose. This first chapter is actually a review of the DVD series, "Linking Your Life to God's Purpose for the World." Both this study guide and the DVD series are part of the "Flourish" package, which enables young people to uncover their God-given purpose in life.

If you have watched the DVD series, this chapter will serve as a reminder before you go forward building a healthy, purposeful lifestyle. If you have not seen the DVD series, be sure and participate in the exercise in this chapter before you progress.

UNCOVERING YOUR PURPOSE
I wandered through my first two years of college. I had a double major because I couldn't make up my mind between the two. I was involved in four ministries on and off the campus in an attempt to figure out what my spiritual gifts were. On top of that, I was working two jobs. I was very busy, but I had a limited sense of focus. My purpose was diluted. Lots of activity—not much accomplishment. Everyone was giving me advice and I didn't know who to listen to.

My world at that point could be summarized by a true story from the 19th century. It's the story of General Taylor and Senator Atchison. Taylor led U.S. troops in several military campaigns, including the Mexican War. Although his men were outnumbered four to one, he outmaneuvered the enemy and won the war. At that point, General Taylor won national acclaim. He was a celebrity of sorts. At 62 years old, however, he decided it was time to quit. So, he rode his horse from Texas to Louisiana to retire at his estate.

Upon his arrival, he was shocked to see his front porch filled with mail. Most of the letters were congratulations on his military success. However, because the postal system was so new, most of the letters arrived with postage due. General Taylor had a decision to make. Did he want to read the letters badly enough to pay for them? He opened a few and each of them said about the same thing—so he determined he would return the entire stack to the dead letter office back in Washington D.C.

That would have been the end of the story if it weren't for a friend who spoke to him two weeks later. His friend asked him if he'd received a letter from Washington, D.C. He laughed and said he'd just sent hundreds of letters back to the capitol, but didn't notice any letter from there. His friend urged him to retrieve the letters and go through them at once. When he did, Taylor found the letter his friend was referring to—it was a letter from his political party inviting him to be their candidate for President of the United States! Within months, Zachary Taylor became the next president of our country.

Believe it or not, there's more. Zachary Taylor's inauguration was scheduled to take place on a Sunday at noon. Taylor was a deeply committed Christian–and he insisted that his inauguration take place on Monday, not Sunday. By law, President Polk could not serve one more day as president. Consequently, the U.S. Senate was forced to choose a man to serve as president from noon on Sunday to noon on Monday. They chose David Rice Atchison. However, because the last days of the Polk administration had been so hectic, Atchison went to bed in the wee hours of Sunday morning, instructing his landlady not to wake him up for any reason. She didn't. Senator Atchison slept through Sunday afternoon, all through Sunday night, all through Monday morning, waking up at about 2:00 p.m. on Monday afternoon. In short, he slept through his entire term of office!

The story of Zachary Taylor and David Rice Atchison furnishes us with a couple of analogies. Do you ever feel like Taylor, inundated with so many voices (sometimes voices of flattery like the letters on his porch), that you're distracted from the one Voice you should be listening to for your next step in life? (So often, God is merely one Voice in the midst of hundreds clamoring for our attention). In addition, do you sometimes feel like Atchison, so weary from the day-to-day grind that you slumber through

---

Is it possible, in the rat race we live in, to live a life on purpose?

Is it possible to play offense and not just defense?

After graduation, can we really hope for a life that consists of more than just maintaining and surviving until the weekend?

opportunities that come your way? (He had the chance to be president for a day!)

So many students today are lost in a world of noise, trying to figure out where they fit. The question that surfaces over and over is: Is it really possible, in the rat race we live in, to live life on purpose? Is it possible to play offense and not just defense? After graduation, can we really hope for a life that consists of more than just maintaining and surviving until the weekend—paying the bills and doing the laundry, waiting for some chance to make a difference in the world? Can we do more than just react to the overload of activities that are thrown at us?

I believe we can. I believe its possible to live life on purpose—and be proactive, not just reactive to opportunities around us. This session will set the stage for that kind of life after you finish college. It will enable you to live a focused life by uncovering the core of God's identity (the One who made you), and the core of your identity. It will provide an exercise that will equip you to link your life to God's purposes for the world, and live the life you were meant to live.

A BIBLICAL FOUNDATION

Before going further, let's lay a foundation. God's Word says:

1. We all have been given a purpose for our lives. God didn't merely call pastors or missionaries to be purposeful about their mission. This call is for everyone. Romans 11:29 reminds us that *"God's gracious gifts and calling are irrevocable."* That means God gives them to all of us—and He doesn't take them back. You can disobey God's call of your life, but you will still answer to Him on it one day.

2. We are most fulfilled when we are fulfilling our purpose. I've found that the closer I get to fulfilling my God-given purpose in life, the measure of fulfillment I experience goes up. It is directly proportionate to my alignment with God's call on my life. If you constantly have days that are empty and dreary, you are not likely to be near to His ultimate calling for you. You may be preparing for that call, but you are not experiencing it. Ephesians 4:1 challenges us to "walk worthy of the calling you have received."

3. Not everyone uncovers their God-given purpose. People don't automatically discover their calling in life. I know folks who've been in church for 50 years and never figured it out. Jesus told a story in Matthew 25 about the talents. In the parable, the master gave one man one talent, another two talents, and a third five talents. Then the master left on a trip. When he returned, he asked the men to give an account for what they'd done with their talents. The last man's story was different. He had buried his talent and done nothing with it. It's interesting to note that we never see God getting angrier with His people (not prostitutes, not thieves, or murderers) than He does with this servant who did nothing with what he'd been given. Think about it. The man didn't lose his talent, he just didn't use it. This is sobering. If you choose to play it safe and never venture out, you may never fulfill your purpose.

4. Our purpose is built from our personal inward wiring. We don't simply conjure up a statement of purpose for our lives. We uncover the purpose that is already inside of us. God has wired you with spiritual gifts, burdens, passions, talents, and a certain background and personality that are unique. Once you see how those all fit together, you can begin to uncover your purpose according to God's plan for your life. Psalm 139 reminds us that God knit our inward parts together in secret long ago, and from them, we become distinctive individuals. Our goal should be to discover what God has deposited inside of us.

5. We will be judged on our obedience to our God-given calling in life. The New Testament speaks of two judgments. The great white throne judgment is where God will judge humankind for their sin. Believers have already passed through that judgment. However, we have stepped into another judgment, called the judgment seat of Christ (2 Cor. 5:10). This one is not about sin—but about whether we have walked in the Spirit and obeyed God's calling on our lives. It is about our behavior, not our nature. Did we do what we were designed to do?

REFLECT AND RESPOND

1. Stop and reflect for a moment. Do you have any idea what God's purpose for your life is? Obviously, He's called all of us to love others and make disciples, but how are you different from others around you? How specific can you be about your purpose?

2. Which of the five foundations above is most gripping to you?

HOW GOD REVEALED PURPOSE IN SCRIPTURE

Through the ages God has called out men and women for His purposes. Some followed, others didn't. As I review the pages of Scripture, I notice four common ways God used to communicate a "life purpose" to individuals. Obviously, He's not bound to these four methods today. See if you identify with any of these people in the Bible:

Thunderbolt–This is when God reveals your purpose in life in a moment, or a single event. Perhaps it's at a special event, or during your quiet time, but in that period, God seems to clarify your calling. The apostle Paul experienced this type of calling. He was on the road to Damascus when Jesus spoke to him, transformed him, and defined his calling. In that single event, Saul became Paul, and had a clear sense of his calling.

Walking Through Open Doors–Instead of revealing your purpose in a single step, God may do it over time, through many steps. Esther is a good example. She walked through doors of opportunity to become queen of Persia. Over time she continued taking steps. Eventually, she confronted the king on Haman's plot to kill the Jews—and she helped save the Jewish race. She realized her purpose over the years as she obeyed God each step of the way.

Call From Birth–This calling comes early in life when you intuitively seem to know what you are supposed to do. As a child, God spoke to Jeremiah and told him that before he was in his mother's womb, he was called and ordained to be a prophet to the nations. If you could talk to Jeremiah, he would say he had always known his calling from childhood.

Growing Awareness–This call generally comes to young adults. God lays out the big picture of your purpose, but gives few details. As you begin to walk toward that calling, the details get filled in. Joseph is an example. In Genesis, he had a dream as a teenager about being a leader. As he re-

---

Four common ways God used to communicate "life purpose" to individuals

1. Thunderbolt

2. Walking Through Open Doors

3. Call From Birth

4. Growing Awareness

Can you identify?

mained faithful over time, God guided the fulfillment of that dream. He led in Egypt and kept the Jewish race alive during seven years of famine.

TRY THIS OUT!

1. Do you identify with any of these ways that God called individuals? Be prepared to share which one you identify most clearly with.

2. How does God usually speak to you and give you direction in life?

THE EXERCISE

OK, here it is. For the rest of this session, I will walk you through an exercise to enable you to uncover your God-given purpose. At least you'll get closer to understanding it. Let's begin with a list of ingredients involved in understanding your purpose. Do you remember that I told you that your purpose is built from your personal inward wiring? These are the issues you should think about as you decipher your inward wiring. Respond to the following questions:

1. NATURAL TALENTS: What abilities do you possess?
Inside each of us, God placed innate abilities. Some are harder to find than others. List some of the abilities you've had, even before you became a Christian. (Exodus 31:1-11).

2. SPIRITUAL GIFTS: What is your primary spiritual gift?
Every believer has a spiritual gift. A list of gifts is found in Romans 12:6-8. Others are found in Ephesians 4:10-11, 1 Corinthians 12:4-11 and 1 Peter 4:10-11.

3. INWARD DESIRES: What do you want to do with your life?
I used to think God's will would automatically be something I'd have to suffer through. His Word says, "Take delight in the Lord, and He will give you your heart's desires." (Psalm 37:4; See also Philippians 2:13).

4. RESULTS & FRUIT: What produces the most when you do it?
As you look around at the activities in which you participate, which ones

really bear fruit? What seems to come natural for you, you're good at it, and it gets results?

5. AFFIRMATION & RECOGNITION: What do close friends affirm about you?
Sometimes we are too close to our situation to see it objectively. Listen to friends who know you well and know God well. What do they affirm about your strengths?

6. CONVICTIONS & PASSION: What convictions are you compelled to pursue?
Are there any issues that burn inside of you? Is there a cause that you believe someone ought to do something about that? What is it? Jot it down in a shortened form in the margin.

7. FULFILLMENT & SATISFACTION: What do you deeply enjoy doing?
Can you identify those activities that bring you the deepest sense of fulfillment? What makes you come alive? What would you do even if you had to do it for free?

8. CIRCUMSTANCES & OPPORTUNITY: What are your opportunities now?
What is in front of you right now that might be a God-given opportunity, if you could only see it? Are there recurring opportunities that might be a divine appointment?

Before going forward, look back at your responses to these questions. Do you see any patterns? Are there any thoughts that keep coming up? This might be a tip-off to help you to discover your God-given mission.

GUIDELINES FOR YOUR PURPOSE

Have you ever been in a city and noticed pigeons walking around a park? They look funny because they move their heads back and forth with every step they take. Do you know why they do this? I read research on those birds and found out they move their heads as they walk to adjust their perspective. They can see things more clearly if they make such adjustments with each step. Hmmm. Maybe we can learn something from pigeons. Perhaps we should adjust our perspective on life before we take our next step.

Any purpose that reflects God will include others in it.

It will always involve serving people in some way.

My goal is to enable you to write a statement of purpose for your life. Before you walk through the questions that will help you get started, let me pause for a moment, and give you some perspective. The following are a handful of guidelines that will help you keep your purpose statement aligned with God, and not become simply your own idea. If you plan to uncover God's purpose for your life, this list will guide you.

YOUR PURPOSE OUGHT TO...

1. Begin with God's priorities.–As ironic as it may sound, your purpose doesn't start with you. It's not about your agenda but about God's purposes on earth. Therefore, your purpose ought to begin with the great commandment and the Great Commission. (Matthew 22:37-29; 28:19-20). This is what every believer's purpose will have in common. Ask God: "What are You doing in the world, and how can I link my life to what You are already doing?"

2. Revolve around your identity.–Once you begin with God's agenda, you should make sure your purpose statement revolves around your identity—your passions, gifts and personality. Remember the list of eight personal ingredients you noted above? They make up your identity. This makes the purpose statement unique to you; it reflects the burdens and passion God has given you.

3. Include others.–Any purpose statement that reflects God will include others in it. It will always involve serving people in some way. I can't imagine that God's purpose for you could be fulfilled in isolation. It will always be for the benefit of others. What we do for ourselves dies with us. What we do for others lives on. You cannot fulfill this purpose alone. This has implications for you in college and when you enter the workforce.

4. Be Bigger Than Yourself.–Your purpose should take a lifetime to fulfill. It cannot be accomplished in a few years. In fact, it will be challenging enough that you feel you cannot pull it off without God. Richard Bach is said to have been asked how we know if our purpose is completed. He responded: "If you are alive, it isn't."

5. Contain life-changing convictions.–Only if you have something worth dying for—do you really have something worth living for. It is nothing to die. It is an awful thing to have never lived. Your purpose ought to include words and ideas that capture the essence of your beliefs.

6. Have eternal value.–Eternity should be affected in some way by the fulfillment of your purpose. While I believe in social justice and political involvement, those alone aren't enough to fulfill God's purpose for you. Our goal should not be to fulfill our purpose, make life better for some, and still allow people to end up in hell. Don't limit your purpose to simply moving things around here on planet earth.

A LITTLE PERSPECTIVE

I remember watching the Rose Bowl a few years ago on January 1st. A college student who had helped to build floats out of flowers all four years of his college career had won yet another award for his work. A reporter asked him if he enjoyed working on the floats. He responded by saying it was the highlight of his year each year. But when the reporter asked if he could envision doing it as a career, he replied: "No way."

This surprised the reporter a bit, so she persisted and asked why not. In response, the student gave a remarkably insightful comment. He said: "Because I cannot imagine giving so much of myself to something that is thrown into the garbage a week later."

Interesting. This student may not have even been a Christian, but he had a clear idea that he wanted to invest himself into something that mattered. Something that wasn't temporary. I wonder how many students who say they believe in God, have given their lives, by default, to some temporary vision that won't matter a few years from now.

CHECKLIST FOR YOUR PURPOSE STATEMENT

Now we're ready for the exercise. At least, I hope you are ready. Now that you've looked inside yourself, and you've reviewed the guidelines for aligning your purpose statement to the heart of God, let's examine 10 issues that will direct you in writing a statement of purpose for your life. The following list could be called: "Life Planning in Ten Steps."

It's designed for you to respond during an extended block of solitude time. I suggest you carve out a D.A.W.G. (Day Alone With God), and take this lesson with you - along with your Bible, a notepad and a pencil. After each of the 10 issues, take some time and write in your responses as honestly as you can. Think and pray over each of them. Then, look for patterns in your answers. Once again, do you see a common thread in what you've written? What do you discover about yourself?

I wonder how many students around you who say they believe in God have given their lives, by default, to some temporary vision that won't matter in a few years?

Fasten your seatbelts and get ready to reflect and respond to God's purposes for your life.

1. Burdens–What needs tug most at your heart? What are the things which make you cry or angry, or cause you to become passionate? Do you ever watch the news and get upset over certain stories, and feel like someone ought to do something about it?

2. Hallmarks–What are the major hallmarks that make up your life? Are there any markers that seem to indicate your destiny? List significant books, mentors, accomplishments, events, and people that have shaped you into who you are today. They can be both positive and negative hallmarks that have made an impression on you.

3. Themes–What recurring themes or issues seem to keep coming up in your conversations or Bible studies? Are there subjects you return to regularly? Step back and listen to yourself for a few days. What are your mega-themes that might be a tip-off of what your mission ought to revolve around.

4. Tools and Resources–What specific resources do you have at your side that you could employ as you fulfill your mission? These tools could be possessions like a computer, people such as friends or classmates, or skills such as an ability you have to persuade people or plan effectively. List your tangible assets.

5. Style–What's your personality profile? What do you learn when you collect the results from spiritual gifts tests? Personality tests? Style of influence profiles? Motivational needs surveys? List the cumulative results here and compare. Are you an outgoing activist? Are you a plodder or a planner? Are you a team builder? Describe yourself: what special style do you use to reach your goals?

6. Dreams–What are some of your aspirations or ideas that could become a God-given clarified vision in the future? What are the things you'd love to do or be? You may want to write a paragraph or draw a picture, but describe some of the dreams you might attempt to fulfill if you had no fear of failure.

7. Mission–This is it. Each item has hopefully led you to this point of declaring your statement of mission. Write your mission statement that answers: Why do I exist? Why did God give me to the world? Write out the central purpose of your life in one to three questions.

8. Vision–Based on your mission, describe in detail what you see as the ultimate results of your life. You might have several visions to accomplish in your personal, family, or career life that all fit who you are, and all complement your purpose. Write them as if you were seeing your contribution from the other end of your life. Start the statements with the words: I see…

9. Core Values–Once you've written a mission and vision statement, it is helpful to list the inner-based principles that drive you. These hidden factors can be defined as single words of belief. They are descriptions of who you are or who you want to become. Words such as integrity, or servant's heart, or mentor, and so forth. These words will be the horsepower behind the major decisions you make in the future. What are the principles or values that drive you as you live out your life on campus, in the community, in your church?

10. Goals and Objectives–Finally, list the areas in which you will need to stay involved on a regular basis, if you hope to accomplish your mission. This category is important because it will enable you to translate your purpose into a "to do" list for Monday morning. What steps will you take this week and beyond to reach your major goals?

- **Lifetime Goals** – What you want to see happen over the long haul?
- **Mid-range Goals** – What you want to see happen in one to five years?
- **One-year Goals** – What you want to see happen this year?
- **90-Day Goals** – What you want to see happen in the next three months?
- **Next Steps** – What must go on your to-do list today to get started?

NOTE: Write your responses to the 10 issues on a pad of paper, or use a large sheet of paper where everything you want to express can fit on one page.

MY ATTEMPT AT A PURPOSE STATEMENT

Although writing a purpose statement may seem intimidating, I actually first wrote mine during my sophomore year of college. At 19 years of age I put on paper that I wanted to "influence the influencers" and be part of a "global ministry."

At the time I was not doing anything spectacular. I was involved in volunteer ministry opportunities on the streets and in a local prison. I soon took a part-time youth pastor position. Later I moved into a full-time pastoral position in San Diego, working with John Maxwell–an even larger opportunity to impact people. Years later, I moved to Denver, where I worked with a national ministry across the U.S. Next, I worked with a ministry called EQUIP, a worldwide ministry where I equipped leaders. Currently, I direct a ministry called Growing Leaders that is committed to influencing young leaders around the world. Sound familiar? I believe I may now be fulfilling the purpose God began to reveal to me as a 19-year-old college student.

Everyone's purpose statement will look a little different because God made us all unique. (We only have the great commandment and the Great Commission in common.) Let me offer you my mission statement as an example of what one might look like. Please don't imitate it. I just want it to encourage you to make yours as big and specific as possible. Here is mine:

As a friend and follower of Jesus, I purpose to be a catalyst for the world through: Evangelizing the lost–I want to impact one million people for Christ by sharing my God-given gifts and grace. Equipping leaders–I want to influence the influencers by creating tools and training experiences for leaders. Enlisting laborers–I will invest my l i f e and multiply workers through mentoring others to find their mission.

YOUR ATTEMPT AT A PURPOSE STATEMENT
Jot down your early attempt at a statement of purpose for your life:

THE DAY-TO-DAY GRIND
Before we ask any more questions, let's pause and examine how to translate this life purpose stuff into our day-to-day grind. Spend a day and tabulate what consumes your time in the weekly routine of life. Often, we need to insert purpose into our schedules, or we'll be overcome with trivia. This will help us live our lives on purpose. When we do this, our life becomes a wild and wonderful adventure—with God at the steering wheel.

Everyone's purpose statement will look a little different because God made us all unique.

> *I covered the whole gospel, and God used it. I got to share Christ with three million New Zealanders at the 5:00, 6:00, and 11:00 news that evening.*

I discovered this while in New Zealand in 1990. By that time I was working to live my life on purpose, every minute of the day. I was working with Youth For Christ for two weeks doing student crusades. After a stellar first week on the north island, our team flew down to the south island for a second week. On that flight I read an article about New Zealand's poor spiritual condition. I became burdened thinking about this and prayed this prayer: "Lord, help me to impact not only this next camp, but this whole country!" (I often pray stuff like this and have no idea what I'm inviting God to do.)

God answered my prayer: As our four-man team boarded a single engine plane to fly to the campsite, we hit some major gusts of wind. As we attempted to land, our pilot realized he didn't have enough room to land the plane on his first approach, so he'd have to take the plane back up and attempt a second landing. As we tightened our seatbelts, the instrument panel lit up. The engine stalled and our pilot panicked. (You know you are in trouble when the pilot screams while landing the plane!) We began to spiral downward from 120 feet in the air and crash landed. The left wing burst, our wheels flew off, the propeller came off and caught fire, and we spun around several times. It was frightening, but it all happened in a matter of seconds. When we finally stopped, people came running out to us with fire extinguishers. Some put out the flames while others pulled us from the plane. Fortunately, all of us were still alive.

God was up to something. A helicopter arrived to take the other three guys to the emergency unit while I stayed back and nursed my injuries. As I lay resting at a house nearby, my purpose began to unfold. There was a knock at the door. When the host answered, he found news people from the two national television networks. Evidently, our little plane crash was the #1 news story of the day. They asked if anyone there saw the plane crash. My host said, "Saw the plane crash? We have a guy in the back room who was in the plane crash!"

As it turned out, they started the cameras rolling and did an interview with me. They asked me to tell them what happened. Remembering my prayer request earlier about impacting this whole country, I decided this was my opportunity. I began to share about the protection of God and the grace of Jesus. I covered the whole gospel, and God used it. I got to share Christ with three million New Zealanders at the 5:00, 6:00, and

11:00 news that evening. God can turn our worst moments into moments of purpose if we keep our eyes open and our antennas up.

In order to maintain sanity and direction, insert the following into each week:

1. **Contemplation** (Solitary times for study, prayer ,and meditation)
2. **Community** (Participation in a small group for accountability and support)
3. **Calling** (Doing something about your ultimate calling, based on your statement)
4. **Celebration** (Refueling your life with friends and family)

ASKING THE RIGHT QUESTION

I have often said, the most popular extracurricular activity for Christian students is a game you might call: "Finding the ideal, perfect, private, desirable will of God for my life." Typically, this game begins with the question, *"What do I want and what will God let me have?"*

Unfortunately, this question will not lead to uncovering your God-given purpose. We cannot find God's will by starting with the self-preoccupied question from the land of evermore: *What do I want and what will God let me have?* Instead, we must begin with the kingdom questions: *What does God want? What is He doing in history? How can I link my life to His purposes for the world today?*

If you've had a challenging time engaging in this life-purpose exercise, I suggest you begin with the questions below. They will help you get started, and may feel less intimidating. They are "big picture" questions as you live your life on campus and in the workforce:

1. God, what are You doing in history? What are Your purposes for the world?
2. What is my earliest memory of God's call on my life?
3. What has God been saying to me through His Word, over the long haul?
4. What has God been saying to me through the needs and suffering of others?
5. What is God saying to me through my gifts and abilities?

6. What is God saying to me through the broken places in my life?
7. What is God saying to me through my imagination?
8. What is God saying to me through my community (those who know me best)?
9. What is God saying to me through my active research?
10. How does my calendar today reflect my understanding of God's purpose for me?
11. How can I inject purpose into my weekly agenda?
12. Who can hold me accountable to progress toward fulfilling my sense of purpose?
13. When is it time to get started, and what should I do first?

CHANGING YOUR OBITUARY

Near the end of the 19th century, a Swedish chemist named Alfred woke up one morning, and stumbled into the kitchen to read the morning paper. Doing so, he got a major wake-up call. He was shocked to read his own obituary in the paper!

After careful thought, he realized that the journalists had confused him with his brother who had recently passed away. However, he decided to take advantage of the moment, and actually read what the paper wrote about his life. Here's what he read:

Alfred Nobel, the inventor of dynamite, who died yesterday, devised a way for more people to be killed in a war than ever before, and he died a rich man.

Reading his account had a profound affect on Alfred. He decided he wanted to be known for something other than developing the means to kill people efficiently and for amassing a fortune in the process. So, he initiated the Nobel Peace Prize, the award for scientists and writers who foster peace. Years later, Nobel commented: "Every man deserves a chance to change their obituary in midstream and write a new one."

Do you know what I have attempted to do in this chapter for you? I want to give you a chance to change your obituary toward the beginning of your life.

Do you know what I have attempted to do in this session for you? I want to give you a chance to change your obituary toward the beginning of your life.

ASSESSMENT

Think about what you possess inside of you that might be a tip as to your life purpose. In the space below, jot down anything that pops into your mind.

APPLICATION

Based on the previous list, write in pencil a purpose statement for your life.

DEEPENING YOUR INTIMACY WITH GOD

Experiencing Intimacy with God Will Increase Your Influence for God

"My goal is to know Him and the power of His resurrection and the fellowship of His sufferings, being conformed to His death, assuming that I will somehow reach the resurrection from among the dead."
(Philippians 3:10-11)

"This is eternal life; that they may know You, the only true God, and the One You have sent – Jesus Christ."
(John 17:3)

When an Elvis Presley look-alike contest came to Massachusetts, the Boston Globe was on the scene. A story in the newspaper spotlighted a certain fan. Listen to his comments. I think they are quite insightful:

"Presley was and is my idol. I've seen his concerts, I have every album he has recorded, and watched every movie he's made. I once got a hair contour like his, and now I have a face-lift just like his…I have won Elvis look-alike contests dozens of times…I have ticket stubs and clippings from programs around the world; I even own some Elvis pillows from Japan.

"On several occasions I wanted him to see me, so I would storm the stage, before and after the concerts he would do. I don't think he ever noticed. I once even climbed the walls around Graceland, the Presley mansion. I think it might have been him wandering through the house as I looked through my binoculars, but I'm not sure. It's really funny. All the effort I put into following him . . . and I could never seem to get close."

Hmmm. How despondent. There's an analogy in this article for you and me. How many times have we felt this way about our experience with God? We go to Bible studies, pray, sing the songs, and even lift our hands. Yet, if we are honest about it, at times we've all felt the same way this fan felt about his idol, Elvis Presley: "It's funny…all the effort I put into following Him…and I could never get close."

SESSION 2

25 - FLOURISH

INTIMACY

Intimacy. People are talking about it more and more these days. Intimacy in marriages. Intimacy among friends. And, most of all—intimacy with God. We seek relationships that will fill our need for closeness. The ultimate relationship is with God. I have found that people around the world long to experience Him in a genuine way, and will follow leaders who create a place for that to happen.

So, why don't we do this? Why is the issue of intimacy with God so mystical and elusive?

IN THE BEGINNING...

To get to the root of our dilemma, let's travel back to the Book of Genesis. Adam was the first spiritual leader in the world. Scripture says he was to lead Eve, his wife, as well as to take dominion of the earth and maintain the garden. When he sinned, the human race took on a new nature and bent toward independence from God. Their intimacy with God was shattered. It would require radical and reciprocal measures to recapture it again. This event was the beginning of the struggle for intimacy with God that we still face today. Note the impact of sin on humanity's intimacy with God. Our sinful nature causes us to...

1. Keep A Distance From God

Instead of walking with God in the cool of the day, Adam and Eve hid from Him. Rather than pursuing their Creator with all of their hearts, they fled from Him in shame. Sin puts a chasm between God and us. We find it easier to be separated from God than pursue Him. Most of us experience this strange hide-and-seek game with God due to our nature (Genesis 3:8-10).

2. Disobey God

Our sinful nature causes us to desire independence from God and others. We disobey naturally. Originally, Adam relied upon God to set the agenda for his life. When he ate the forbidden fruit, it was his first independent act apart from God. Today, we also desire independence from God. It's difficult to consistently make God's desires our desires (Genesis 3:11-13).

3. Withhold our affections from God

Adam had the privilege of actually walking with God daily. He experienced God at the most intimate level. But after he chose to disobey he was afraid to be vulnerable. The first emotion Adam felt after he sinned was fear. The emotional intimacy was broken. For us, we will not risk intimacy if we are afraid of rejection or indifference (Genesis 3:10).

4. Avoid responsibility for our state

Now that Adam and Eve had something to hide from God, they were faced with the new desire to avoid taking responsibility for their actions. Adam blamed Eve and God for his actions, which further strained his intimacy with God. Eve blamed the serpent for her behavior. Their shame led to blame (Genesis 3:12-13).

MAKE YOURSELF AT HOME

Compare your relationship with God to a house. When you first invited Christ to come in to your heart and began your journey with Him, it could be compared to entering the front door, and coming in from the cold outside. Do you remember how it first felt? Maybe you were excited. Maybe you were unsure. Maybe you were curious—but it felt good to be inside the house, didn't it? Even though you were just in the entrance foyer of the house, at least you were inside. You were just glad to be there. Later, however, you may have noticed something. The novelty wore off. Your Christian life became more of a routine. It was in those times, that God was motioning you to explore the other rooms of the house: the den, the kitchen, the family room. He was beckoning you to continue the search.

What did you do? Sadly, most Christians respond this way: "Oh, Lord, I'm perfectly content in the entrance foyer. I'm just happy to be here." And they remain in the entrance foyer of their salvation experience for their entire lives.

REFLECT AND RESPOND

When was the last time you disobeyed God? After your disobedience, what affections did you withhold from Him? After you realized your sin, did you take responsibility for your actions? Or did you avoid responsibility by placing blame on someone else or making excuses such as, "That's just one of my weaknesses," or "It's no big deal. God will forgive me"?

Discuss with another Christian your comments and thoughts related to these questions.

Intimacy with God can be difficult to understand because it often seems awe-inspiring, mystical, ambiguous, and subjective.

COMMON BARRIERS TO INTIMACY

This independent nature makes intimacy difficult and foreign to us—with God and each other. This opposition against God introduces a new set of barriers that frequently prevent us from experiencing an intimate relationship with God.

1. **Unconfessed sin and disobedience**
2. **Negative self-esteem and insecurity**
3. **Poor models of intimacy growing up**
4. **Unforgiveness**
5. **A driven spirit**
6. **Distrust**

Intimacy with God can be difficult to understand because it often seems awe-inspiring, mystical, ambiguous and subjective. Our understanding of this relationship comes from several key thoughts from the New Testament. Intimacy with God can be defined as:

Pursuing God in order to experience the PROMISE of Ephesians 3:18-19 and the COMMAND of Matthew 22:37, which results in the FRUIT of John 15:15-16.

SQUEEZE YOUR OWN JUICE...

Read Ephesians 3:18-19. What is the reward of intimacy with God? Jot your thoughts below.

Read Matthew 22:37. What is the responsibility of intimacy with God? Briefly jot your thoughts in the space below.

Read John 15:15-16. What is the result of intimacy of God? Briefly share your thoughts with another Christian.

REFLECT AND RESPOND

Reflect on someone with whom you experience healthy intimacy? What intimate experiences characterize that relationship? Compare this relationship to the one you have with God. What are the similarities? What are the differences?

MYTHS ABOUT INTIMACY

Intimacy with God is often a misunderstood concept. Here are six common myths. Circle "Yes" or "No" after each one, based on whether you've ever struggled with the lie.

The Feelings Myth   Yes   No

If I feel spiritual, I must be close to God.
Truth: Many people involved in the New Age Movement (dated? Scientology?) feel close to God, yet they are not truly intimate with Him. It's all a feeling, not based on biblical truth.

The Knowledge Myth   Yes   No

I know so much Scripture; I must be close to God.
Truth: Even though atheists know Scripture, they do not experience intimacy with God. Jesus got more upset with the religious Pharisees than He did with the prostitutes!

The Emotion vs. Truth Myth   Yes   No

If I feel badly, I must not be intimate with God.
Truth: If our relationship with God were truly based on emotion, it would have been over long ago. King David felt horrible as he repented of his sin with Bathsheba, yet he was never closer to God than in that act of repentance.

The Good Deeds Myth   Yes   No

If I work at doing good, I know I'm close to God.
Truth: Intimacy with God will not be achieved through accomplishing a spiritual checklist. Many claim that they are saved by grace, but they continue to cling to their righteous acts as if they are the justifying force for their acceptance.

The Positional Myth   Yes   No

Intimacy with God is automatic if I'm "in Christ."
Truth: Being in Christ is automatic if you're a Christian, but abiding in Him is not. There is a difference between our position in Christ and our abiding in Christ. Abiding is a day-to-day experience.

The Intensity Myth   Yes   No

If I serve God with great zeal, I must be intimate.
Truth: Believing that the intensity of our ministry dictates our intimacy level with God is a performance trap. Many people serve God on a short-term mission trip and build a hospital. However, they may confuse intensity for God and intimacy with God.

Many times, these myths seep into our lives without us even knowing it. Slowly, they become foundational to how we relate to God. The more we embrace these myths, the more we put a lid on our capacity to be intimate with God.

REFLECT AND RESPOND
Which of these myths listed are evident in your walk with God? How have these lies affected your intimacy with God? Which would be most relevant to students on your campus?

JESUS' FIVE LEVELS OF INTIMACY
Obviously, we all experience different levels of intimacy with God and each other. Even during Jesus' ministry on earth, He watched people grow into various stages of intimacy with Him.

THE STAGES OF INTIMACY
As we move toward intimacy (whether with people or with God), these general stages are encountered. We progress toward intimacy one-step at a time, as we feel safe.

> **1. Cliché:** Phrases we use out of courtesy, but carry no risk or transparency. When we are least intimate with God, we simply speak to Him in clichés. "Father, bless this food to our bodies" without any understanding of what this means.

When we reach the deepest level of intimacy, we become fully honest and transparent before God.

2. **Facts:** Growing closer by sharing information from our lives. We begin to share facts such as prayer requests for our health, car, or other concrete details in our life. "Father, my car needs a new muffler, and my parents are traveling."

3. **Ideas & Opinions:** Sharing deeper personal thoughts we have on issues. We progress to sharing with God our thoughts about things that happen around us. Father, please help Carrie not to get offended when I share with her."

4. **Feelings:** Opening up to share our emotions, being vulnerable about who we are. We become more intimate, we even share our deep emotions with God. "Father, right now I'm hurting because…"

5. **Total Honesty:** Exhibiting the deepest level of trust by sharing our very life. When we reach the deepest level of intimacy, we become fully honest and transparent before God. "Father, I don't know why You have called me to do this, but I'm relying on You for everything."

REFLECT AND RESPOND

Just as we experience these five stages and levels in human relationships, we experience them in our relationship with God. Discuss how you are experiencing these levels and stages of intimacy with God.

Several years ago, I met Adam when I went to Budapest for a mission trip. In broken English, this 19-year-old communist soldier asked me why I was in his country. I explained that I had traveled with a team, hoping to share about our relationship with God and see if anyone was interested in knowing more about it. At this point I discovered that Adam knew just enough English to cuss me out. He basically told me to take my religion back to America!

As soon as I got back to my tent, I said to my wife, "We've got to pray for Adam. I am going to try to meet with him every day, and I want to be able to share the gospel before I leave." It was hard to communicate with him at first, but over the next three weeks, Adam and I spent nearly every day together. I worked at it. On the final night we sat around a campfire with the team, munching on popcorn. After finishing, Adam and I took a walk.

"Adam," I started, "I feel like I need to apologize for coming on so strong these last three weeks with my Christian faith . . ." He interrupted me. "Oh no, you don't need to apologize. I have thought a lot about God since you have been here. In fact, I have talked to the air twice (that's what he called praying) and both times I got an answer!"

For the next two hours we talked. At the end of the conversation I asked him, "What would keep you from inviting Christ to take over your life?" Through broken English Adam said, "Well, if knowing God means having what you have, I want Him in my life."

A CROSS-CULTURAL RELATIONSHIP

This is a real life picture of why intimacy with God is so difficult. To go from hostility to friendship, Adam and I had to cross the bridges of unfamiliarity, language, worldview, and culture. It took three weeks, a lot of patience, and much determination. Now consider this: our relationship with God requires work because it is a cross-cultural relationship. Think of the daunting gap between God and us! In Isaiah 55:9-11, He said, "My ways are higher than your ways, and My thoughts than your thoughts." If it took so much work to build a friendship between Adam and me, how much more must we devote to God? One reason more people don't experience intimacy with God is that it is simply too much work. Cross-cultural relationships require effort!

A T.H.E.O.L.O.G.Y. FOR INTIMACY

For us to become intimate with God we need to take the necessary steps to understand the essential ingredients for it. It doesn't just happen. There are certain issues to be settled before we will experience an intimate relationship with Him. We will need to stir the following ingredients into the recipe and put ourselves into position to experience Him. Memorize this acronym for the word theology to remind you of what is needed.

T – TIME

We can't experience real closeness with anyone overnight. Time is often the most difficult essential to add. We must give Him time over the long

"Well, if knowing God means having what you have, I want Him in my life."

haul. In other words, our relationship with God forms in a crock-pot, not a microwave oven. If I asked you what elements are necessary to grow a plant in the garden, you would say: soil, seeds, water, sunshine, fertilizer, and so forth. My guess is, you would probably forget the element of time. Plants don't grow overnight—neither do intimate Christ followers. We must daily spend time with God to develop an intimate relationship, over a lifetime.

APPLICATION: I must be patient.
How much time do you spend with your Heavenly Father? Do you need to be investing more time? If so, think about how do you plan to make a change? How will you implement your plan? Share your thoughts with another Christian you trust.

H – HUMILITY
Scripture says that God draws near to the humble but opposes the proud. He loves a broken and contrite heart; that is why intimacy is always preceded by humility. This is illustrated in Jacob's life. God's wrestling match for control of Jacob's life began 20 years before the famous match in Genesis 32:22-31. God had to break him of his deceptive life, and get him to be humble and honest about his need for God. In the same way, God breaks us of self-sufficiency, self-promotion, and self-righteousness. Why? Because He manifests His presence in the holy place and the lowly place (Isaiah 57:15).

APPLICATION: I must be broken.
Do you ever feel that you have wrestled with God as Jacob once did? Who won? Do you have a spirit of humility in your life?

E – EXPRESSION
We will not get close to God or to anyone else unless both parties express themselves in vulnerable, loving ways. Sometimes, it is easier to be more concerned with our image or reputation than in truly expressing our affection to Him with our words, actions, and song. Just as a husband doesn't merely shake hands with his wife, we should not be satisfied with trite and superficial expressions of love to God.

God isn't found through rigidity or through keeping some sort of checklist. Rather, He is found through relational, honest, and transparent approaches to His grace.

I remember learning this when I would return home after a long day at work. My young kids would run to me with their arms up, smiles on their faces and yelling: "Daddy!" This is probably the closest expression of worship I've seen—and illustrates how God would love for us to connect with Him.

APPLICATION: I must learn to worship.
How have you felt God express His love to you? How do you express your love for Him?

O – OPENNESS

God isn't found through rigidity or through keeping some sort of checklist. Rather, He is found through relational, honest, and transparent approaches to His grace. Marriage is a good illustration. The couple doesn't pledge to keep laws for each other; they pledge love. When I married my wife, I didn't stand at the front of the church and promise I'd keep some checklist of chores for her. I said I would love, cherish and provide for her. It's a relationship built upon trust. Bingo. For you, your toughest step might be learning to build an intimate relationship with God built on trust. Do you fully trust Him?

APPLICATION: I must trust and be transparent.
Do you feel that you are completely open with God? Is your heart a transparent place where there are no walls? If not, how can the walls be removed?

L – LISTENING

We must learn to listen to His voice if we desire intimacy. We lose intimacy when we stop listening, not when we stop talking. Don't fall into the trap of substituting echoes of God's voice—for God Himself. Many believers like to listen to good teaching online or through podcasts, but these are messages from people, who have listened to God. We should only listen to these once we have listened to God ourselves. They are echoes. We must learn to hear from Him personally. We must dig into His written Word, and learn to "squeeze our own juice." As Richard Foster writes, we must learn to "waste time with God."

APPLICATION: I must invest time in prayer and Bible Study.
It is imperative you take time to listen to God! What has He been saying to you lately? Allow prayer and Bible study to be a conversation between you and God.

O – OBEDIENCE

A desire to please and a willingness to act are pre-requisites to deep friendship. Jesus equated obedience and friendship. He said, "If you love Me — you will obey Me." When we are friends with someone, we learn to love what they love. Here's the princple: Over time, you to tend to become like those you like. My daughter, Bethany, learned to pop microwave popcorn when she was only three years old. Why? Because she knew how much I love popcorn. One night, I came home from work, and she had a bag all ready for us to eat together. We sat down on the sofa in our family room and began to munch on it. Neither of us said a word for a few minutes. Then, little Bethany broke the silence. She looked at me and said, "Dad—I'm learning to love popcorn more and more." I loved that moment together because what she was really saying was this: "Dad, I don't really love popcorn naturally…but because you love it, I want to learn to love it." This is a signal of intimacy. It's a signal we should be sending to God. He loves to hear us say something like, "Lord—I don't naturally like those people across the campus, but because you love them, I want to learn to as well. I want to please You more than anything."

APPLICATION: I must act on God's requests.
Is your desire to please God followed by actions of obedience? What recent steps of obedience have you taken in your life? When you remember Jesus saying, "If you love Me, obey Me"–think of ways you obey Him and communicate your intimacy with Him.

G – GRACE

All intimate relationships balance both trust and grace. Both parties must trust each other, but when mistakes or flaws emerge, grace steps in. Grace extends acceptance, when the other person is not perfect, or we don't understand them. That's why we need grace. There are times when we are imperfect—and God gives us grace instead of judgment. There are times when we don't understand Him, and we must extend grace instead of judgment. (Our judgment is always shortsighted anyway!)

Intimacy's foundation is love, not law. It is gratitude, not guilt… we must also realize that God always has His arms open to us… regardless of what we have done.

God is not found by keeping the rules or performing for Him. Intimacy's foundation is love, not law. It is gratitude, not guilt. Just as loving parents don't kick their children out of the family if they fail to obey or do a chore, so we must also realize that God always has His arms open to us . . . regardless of what we have done.

APPLICATION: I must let God love me...period.
How have you experienced God's grace? What does grace look like in your own life? Do you find it easy to accept? God is giving it to you freely every day!

Y – YEARNING

Intimacy doesn't happen automatically – we must desire it more than anything else around us! This passion for God is the most important factor in our intimacy. We must be hungry. Jesus taught that the only appropriate way to enter the kingdom on heaven is with passion. Do you remember His parables? He compared God's kingdom to a treasure chest hidden in a field and to a single pearl of great value. It is something to celebrate and pursue with intense passion. We'll discuss this more in the final session.

APPLICATION: I must desire intimacy more than anything else in life.
Do you find yourself yearning for God? How is your spiritual appetite right now?

REFLECT AND RESPOND

These biblical ingredients are necessary for us to experience passionate intimacy with God. Which of these ingredients do you need to cultivate the most? Specifically, how are you going to develop these elements? With a Christian friend, try to develop a plan or strategy to improve your intimacy with God. When you've finished writing the plan, you should be able to envision how this plan will help (example: I will develop grace by practicing forgiveness of myself and others. I will memorize a verse attesting to the grace of God every week for the next month.) Secure an accountability partner to keep you accountable to implement these actions.

ASSESS YOURSELF

Relationships are difficult to assess because they are fluid and often change. But this is designed to help give you a feel for your intimacy with God. Answer the questions below to give you insight into your current intimacy with God.

Never	Sometimes	Often	
○	○	○	In your spare moments, do you find yourself thinking about Jesus and His purposes in the world and for your life?
○	○	○	Do you consider ways to please Him more than you do others or yourself?
○	○	○	Do you look forward to taking time to spend with Him?
○	○	○	Can you describe Him "with your eyes closed?" (David didn't need to see Him physically to confidently describe His loving kindness, etc. We often hide behind the excuse that we need to see Him to feel close.)
○	○	○	How well do you know His character from Scripture? Can you point to specific times when you "proved" His character in your life?
○	○	○	How frequently do you talk to others about Him?
○	○	○	Is He your best friend?
○	○	○	Do you hide certain things (topics) from Him as you pray about your life, and do you neglect certain areas as you pray? How frequently are you absolutely transparent about where you are?

○	○	○	What kinds of subject matter do you talk to Him about? Do you go beyond rhetoric and facts to intimate, honest feelings?
○	○	○	Do you enjoy worshipping Him and look for new ways to express yourself to Him?
○	○	○	Is your driving hunger to obey Him? Does this show in sacrificial surrender of your preferences to do His bidding?
○	○	○	When you practice a Biblical command, is your motive love for Him, or keeping a checklist of do's and don'ts? Does loving God prompt you?
○	○	○	When you enter seasons of your life that are difficult and uncertain — do you trust Him?
○	○	○	Do you live your life, primarily, from a spiritual posture of "brokenness" and gratitude?
○	○	○	Do you believe you "hear His voice" (John 10:3)?
○	○	○	Have you experienced God as "Abba Father" -- do you think of his as warm and inviting?

Now, add your checkmarks. Every "Often" = 3; every "Sometimes" = 2; and every "Never" = 1

36-48: You're probably "very close" to God; intimacy has begun to grow!
22-35: You have a hunger, but need to mature; keep on growing!
10-21: You may be a bit distant; definitely focus yourself on getting to know Him.

REAL LIFE

I had a missionary friend who was frequently called away from home. It was tough on his family, but it was hardest for his little son. At the train station, the boy would cling to him as if to beg him not to go. Most of the time his dad would appease the boy by bringing him an apple (apples were a rare treat in this country). This would distract the child until after he was able to jump on the train and depart.

One day, when he knew the trip would be especially long, my friend brought two apples to the station. He knew it would be a tough departure. Sure enough, the little boy clamped onto his dad's hand with all of his might. Outside of the passenger car my friend was to board, he said, "Now son, I'm going to be home soon, I promise. But, just to make it better I brought you not one, but two apples."

He jammed them into his son's tiny hands and quickly hopped onto the train. After setting down his luggage, he glanced out the door to see if his son was still there. And he told me that as he looked out the opening of the train, he saw the child still standing in the same place he had left him. The apples had been dropped onto the concrete and he had tears rolling down his cheeks. He heard his little boy whimper, "But daddy, I don't want your apples . . . I want you."

BRINGING IT ALL HOME

I think God is looking for students who will say to Him, "Your answers to prayer are wonderful. But, even if I never got another answer, it would be enough to just know You." It's a pure state I'm talking about. No hidden agendas. Is this your heart's cry?

Look back at the plans you have made throughout this lesson. How are you going to pursue a deeper relationship with God? Commit to carrying out this plan now!

I think God is looking for students who will say to Him, "Your answers to prayer are wonderful. But even if I never got another answer, it would be enough to just know You."

WHO DO YOU THINK YOU ARE?

How Your Identity in Christ Impacts Your Life and Leadership

"If any man be in Christ, he is a new creation; the old things are passed away, behold new things have come."
(2 Corinthians 5:17)

Albert Einstein, as a young man, was not considered especially bright. In fact, he didn't speak until he was four years old. As a student, he actually flunked math class! One day, while standing in line to pay a certain type of tax, his mind wandered far away. After a brief wait, his turn came to pay his taxes. As he stepped up to face the clerk she asked for his name. Einstein just stood there completely silent. Again, she stated, "Sir, we are in a hurry. Please, what is your name?" Silence. For the third time she impatiently sputtered, "Sir, we do not have time for games! Please, what is your name?" Finally he confessed, "I'm so sorry, but for the life of me, I simply cannot remember!" He had to go to the end of the line in hopes that he would remember his name the next time around. What irony! Standing in the tax line that day was a man with the highest I.Q., but he couldn't remember who he was!

WE'RE LIKE EINSTEIN

There's an analogy in that story for us. Albert Einstein suffered from something many Christians are plagued with today – we've forgotten our identity. We say the right phrases and we read the right words from the pages of the Bible, but deep down we don't really know who we are. One ingredient for living a life of influence involves settling this issue. We must be secure in who we are in Christ, and the gifts He's placed inside of us.

This issue is foundational to our personal and leadership development. As we interact with what we read in these pages, the insights have the potential to do the following:

- Change the way we live
- Change the level of confidence we have as we lead others
- Enable us to put our emotional health, our personal security and our identity into the hands of God, making us a more Christ-like influence

"You cannot consistently perform in a manner that is inconsistent with the way you see yourself."
Dr. Joyce Brothers

THE FACTS OF THE MATTER

How we perceive ourselves is one of the determining factors of the quality of our leadership. Joyce Brothers insightfully noted, "You cannot consistently perform in a manner that is inconsistent with the way you see yourself."

- Our self-image is a barrier that must be raised for us to reach our potential.
- We must change our beliefs before we can change our behavior.
- We do not attempt greater things because it does not match our perceived mental image of who we are.

BASIC TRUTH

All spiritual leaders must draw their self-esteem and identity from God rather than from the people they lead.

HOUSTON, I THINK WE HAVE A PROBLEM

Look at the diagram below. The top line represents our God-given potential and the bottom line represents our self-image—the way we see ourselves. The dotted line represents our usual level of behavior or performance. Notice that our performance usually hovers at the level of our self-image. Most of the time we go through life staying within our comfort zone. We tend to resist that which we think is above or below our view of ourselves. Once in a while we become adventurous and pull off something that surprises us. But then we chalk it all up to luck and quickly retreat to a level far below our potential. Somehow, we don't feel we deserve to accomplish that much. We are more at home with performing in an average way. We live at the level our self-image dictates.

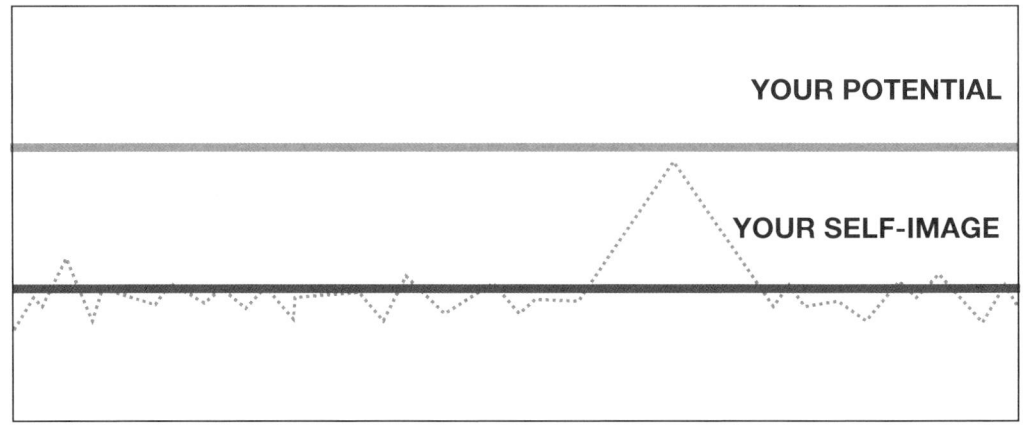

REFLECT AND RESPOND

Write about any specific instances or seasons in your life when you have struggled with your self-image. What was the greatest challenge? How did you overcome it?

Write about one of your bursts of adventure and achievement, and how you were able to live closer to the level of your potential . . .

His background was tough. Raised in the midst of poverty, alcoholism, domestic violence and family illiteracy, Chris was given few reasons to believe that he would ever make much of his life. As a young adult, he struggled to make ends meet with a wife and son to support. He realized that he was fascinated by finance but lacked the connections or education to pursue it. When his wife left, life became even more challenging for Chris as a single parent. Things began to look up when he earned a spot in a competitive stock broker training program. The only catch was that it was an unpaid internship. While completing this program, Chris and his son actually became homeless for several months. Chris continued to purse his dream and not only completed the program but went on to be one the top earners at his firm. You may be familiar with Chris Gardner's story from the film, "The Pursuit of Happyness," where Will Smith portrays his incredible rise from homelessness to success. Through it all, Chris held on to the belief that regardless of where he came from, he could chart a new path and achieve anything he set his mind to.

GET RID OF THE COMMONERS

A low self-image does not happen all by itself. There are hundreds of reasons why individuals struggle with poor self-esteem. Nearly all of us are affected by those reasons. Psychologists tell us that 95% of Americans have a poor self-image by the age of seven. Listed below are some of the common contributors to a low self-image.

REASONS WHY WE'RE OFTEN DOWN ON OURSELVES:

We live in a negative society.
We've seen thousands of murders on TV before we reach high school. We are exposed to divorces, violence and rapes as well. Most news on TV is bad news. Even the weather is reported negatively: there is a 20% chance of rain, instead of an 80% chance of sunshine.

We have had our abilities questioned by others.
Negative words are easily recalled. Positive words are barely remembered. Albert Einstein once remarked that it takes fourteen compliments to displace one criticism.

We confuse failure in a project with failure in life.
We fail at one venture and we say, "I'm a failure," instead of simply realizing we have failed in one area. We forget that failure is an event, not a person.

We often waste time and fail to complete tasks.
Feeling unworthy, we procrastinate on attempting tough challenges. This leads to further discouragement. When we waste time—it deepens the disrespect we have for ourselves.

We make unrealistic comparisons with other's physical features or experiences.
We tend to compare our worst features with someone else's best. Low self esteem makes us tend to compare, compete and condemn others. We feel better when the comparison favors us.

We often have untrained minds.
Whether you know it or not, feeling as though you have a bad memory is a chief cause of a poor self-image. We all have sufficient minds; some are trained and some aren't.

We fail to take care of ourselves.
It's a vicious circle. When we get depressed about something we often

fail to take care of ourselves, which leads to a diminishing self-esteem. We feel unworthy.

We set unrealistic/unreachable standards of perfection.
Sometimes the standards for our appearance (from Hollywood) or for our intelligence (from Harvard) set us up for failure. In reality, we can never be perfect.

We feel that we don't excel at something.
We focus on our weaknesses and are never satisfied with the accomplishments and successes that we have achieved. This is often caused by unfair comparison.

REFLECT AND RESPOND
Can you think of other reasons why you or those you know struggle with self-esteem?

OUR FOUR IMAGES
Our problem is actually even more complex. The truth is, all of us carry the baggage of not one image, but four. We tend to relate to people and conduct ourselves based upon one of the images we are aware of at the moment. Note the diagram below. We enter relationships conscious of how others perceive us. That is the outermost layer. Next, we interact with people attempting to project a certain image to them. , In the next layer we carry with us the actual picture (or image) we have of ourselves. At our very core, deep inside of us, is our true image - the image God has of us.

At our very core, deep inside of us, is our true image – the image God has of us.

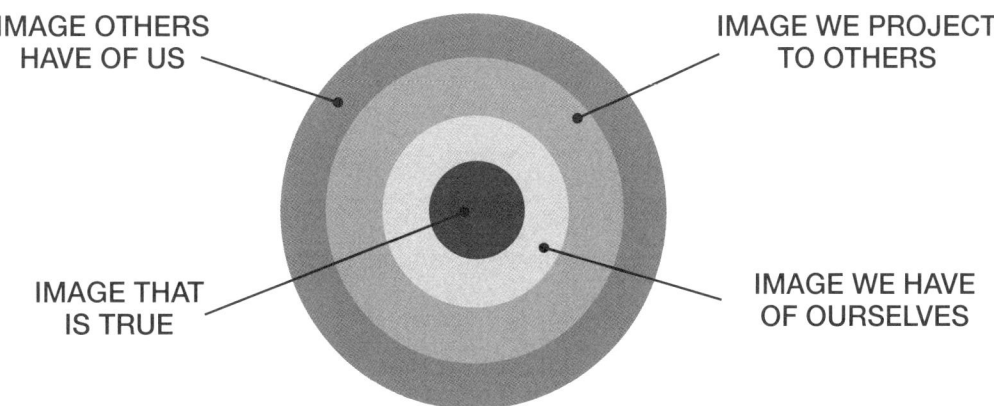

Our job in this chapter is to peel back the three outer layers and live from our true identity: God's image of us! Take a moment and evaluate your self-esteem on the following page.

> "From now on, then, we do not know anyone in a purely human way, yet now we no longer know Him like that. Therefore, if anyone is in Christ, he is a new creation; old things have passed away, and look, new things have come. Now everything is from God, who reconciled us to Himself through Christ, and gave us the ministry of reconciliation."
> 2 Corinthians 5:16-18

REFLECT AND RESPOND

1. I tend to overreact when people tease me.

Never   Seldom   Occasionally   Often   Consistently

2. I am uncomfortable when inactive or alone.

Never   Seldom   Occasionally   Often   Consistently

3. I try to hide the fact that I am down on myself.

Never   Seldom   Occasionally   Often   Consistently

4. I place great emphasis on material possession or beauty.

Never   Seldom   Occasionally   Often   Consistently

5. I usually don't work hard, believing I can't succeed.

Never   Seldom   Occasionally   Often   Consistently

6. I struggle with insecurity, envy and jealousy.

Never   Seldom   Occasionally   Often   Consistently

7. I fear unfamiliar circumstances.

Never   Seldom   Occasionally   Often   Consistently

8. My standards of morality are not especially high.

Never   Seldom   Occasionally   Often   Consistently

Which of the previous responses do you see as weaknesses in your life? Do you notice any other weaknesses not addressed in these eight statements? Write about it in the allotted space on the next page.

LET THE CHANGE BEGIN

Now that we have recognized some of the misconceptions we have about ourselves, let's examine the truth that God reveals in His word. What we need to do is change the picture we have of ourselves based on God's perspective in the New Testament. The truth presented in this text will radically change how we approach our Christian lives.

IT'S GOTTA BE AN INSIDE JOB

Look at 2 Corinthians 5:16-18. Paul is giving us a snapshot of who we are. Think about it. When we asked Christ to come into our lives, we didn't change physically; our height, weight and physical characteristics all remained. Instead, what was dramatically changed was the spirit inside of us. God changes the part of us that is eternal. He did an inside job on us. When God saved us the purpose was to give us a whole new dimension to our identity. We are not just "sinners" saved by grace. We are new creatures in Christ!

Unfortunately, even though we believe God did an inside job on us, most of us don't live from that viewpoint. Instead, we continue to view life through a very human perspective. Let's look at our human way of thought in comparison to our Heavenly Father's perspective.

OUR PERSPECTIVE	GOD'S PERSPECTIVE
We see life, limited by time and space, an existence full of ups and downs.	God sees the big picture – our lives in light of eternity!
Life is based upon our day-to-day experience.	Life is based upon our position in Christ.
We see our flaws and lots of room to grow.	God sees the beauty of His children, complete in Christ.

As we begin to think of our lives in light of God's perspective we realize the limits we often place on ourselves. We long for the indomitable spirit of childhood when we "didn't know any better" than to believe we were special to God and to others.

A little girl stood by the window during a terrible thunderstorm, smiling every time the lightning flashed. Her perplexed father finally asked what she was doing. She giggled, "I think that God's trying to take my picture!"

She understood that her heavenly Father loves her deeply – something we often forget. Not only does God love us but He has also given us some amazing gifts. As we just read in 2 Corinthians, God made us "new creatures." The newness comes with some great benefits! Let's look at three things God has given us: new positions, new possessions and new potential.

God's Perspective: 2 Corinthians 5:16-18

"Because of this decision we don't evaluate people by what they have or how they look. We looked at the Messiah that way once and got it all wrong, as you know. We certainly don't look at him that way anymore. Now we look inside, and what we see is that anyone united with the Messiah gets a fresh start, is created new. The old is gone; a new life burgeons! Look at it! All this comes from God who settled the relationship between us and him, and then called us to settle our relationships with each other." *(The Message)*

YOU HAVE A NEW POSITION

Read 2 Corinthians 5:16-18 again. We are called "new creations" when we are placed in Christ. Something fundamentally changes inside. No longer must we live merely based upon our life on earth, with its ups and downs. We can live based upon our position in Christ.

There was a man who made his living by selling helium balloons on the streets of New York City. Whenever business began to die down he would send one of his colorful balloons zipping into the air and then business would begin to pick up again. One particularly slow day, he let go of several balloons: a red, yellow, and white balloon. It didn't take long before he felt a little tug on his pant leg. Looking down, he discovered a little African-American boy standing there. With child-like innocence he said, "Mister, I have a question . . . if you let go of a black balloon would it go up too?" The man knew just what this boy was getting at. With wisdom beyond his years he bent down and said, "Son, listen to me. It's what is inside those balloons that makes them go up."

When God calls us "new creations," He means it. The Greek term for *new creation* ("new creature" in some versions) literally means "a new species of being that has never existed on earth before." Think about that! When we ask God to come into our lives, it's like God does spiritual surgery. He cuts us open and changes our very being. Therefore, we are a new race – Christians! We must not simply be aware of our new position, we must wholeheartedly embrace it. God wants to infiltrate this planet with a whole new race of people. Not Anglos, Hispanics, Asians or Africans, but a new breed called "new creatures in Christ!" Think about how your life might change if you really believed in your new identity!

God made you a new creature and gave you a new position in Him. Take a moment to compare where you were (or where you would be) without your new position. How has your life changed since you became a new creature?

My old thoughts about my identity . . .   My new thoughts about my identity . . .

A new creation literally means,
"a new species of being that has never existed on earth before."

YOU HAVE NEW POSSESSIONS

2 Corinthians 5:17-18 says, "old things have passed away and look, new things have come. Now everything is from God." What old and new things was Paul speaking of? Read 2 Peter 1:3-4: "His divine power has given us everything we need for life and godliness through our knowledge of him who called us by his own glory and goodness. By these He has given us his very great and precious promises, so that through them you may participate in the divine nature, escaping the corruption in the world caused by evil desires."

Did you catch what Peter said? God has given us "everything" we need to live out our calling as new creatures. We have the opportunity to "participate in the divine nature" so we can be like Jesus. God doesn't want us to merely exist as Christians so we can get into heaven. He wants to make us look like Jesus so we can fit into heaven.

When I was in college I decided to create a diagram of who God said I was "in Christ." I wanted to see all these "things" that both the apostle Paul and Peter said I had. This diagram is what I drew and put on my bathroom mirror in the dorm. It displays some of the key "resources" or "equipment" God has placed inside of us. Check it out.

What might happen if every morning you woke up and saw a "new creature" in Christ?

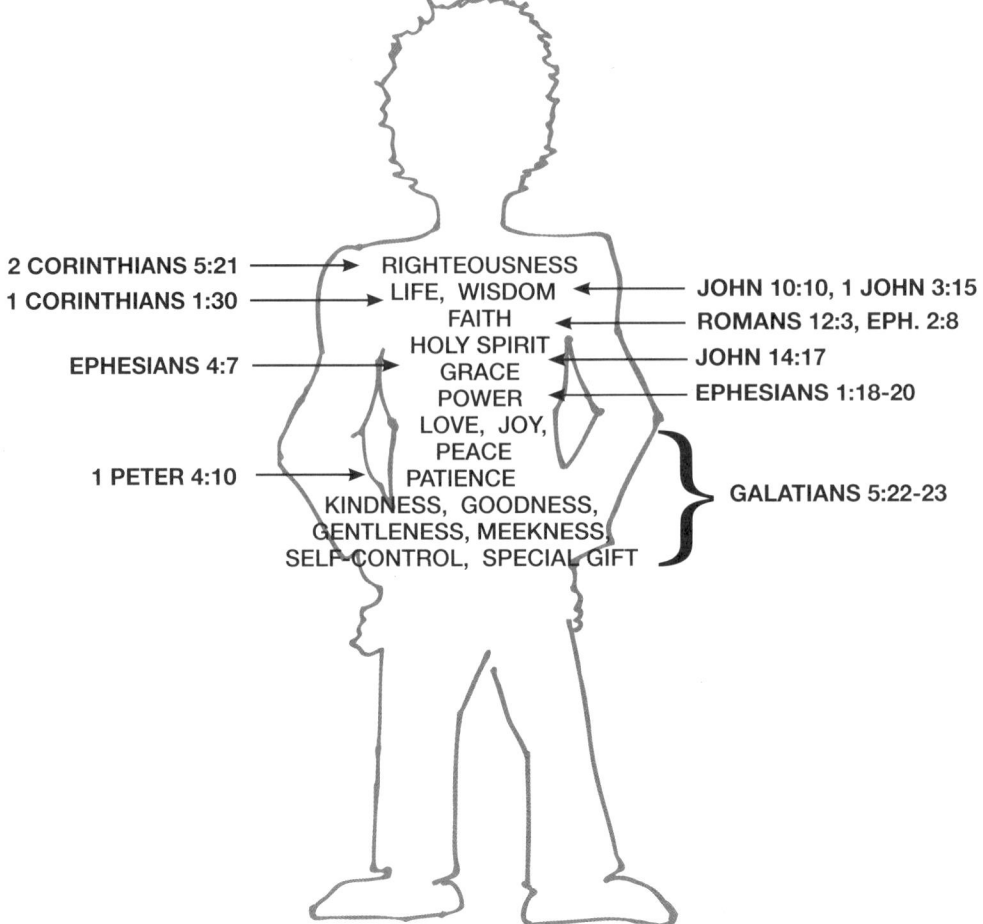

This diagram is a great thing to keep nearby so you can remember who you are each day. Confess each "resource" and Scripture aloud. Some call this brain washing. I agree . . . it sure is! Let's wash our brains clean of the junk that the world has told us and remember the possessions that God has given us. Make your own diagram and put it on your mirror!

Over and over again, I have watched the power of these God-given gifts inside of me. God has literally equipped us to carry on the works of Jesus (John 14:12). When I was in college, I became burdened to "influence the influencers" as I mentioned in Session 1. In my freshman year, I began to pray for celebrity athletes and musicians who were influencing the culture at the time. As I prayed I became burdened with their need for Christ. Someone needed to share Christ with them!

One evening as I prayed for the heavy metal band, KISS, God impressed upon me that I should go beyond my prayer time, and share Christ with them! I was certain it was just bad pizza that I ate the night before, but I couldn't get away from the idea. Later that year they did a concert in town, and God opened up a door for me to talk to them at their hotel. It was one of the scariest things I have ever done, but what kept me there was the truth I am sharing in this chapter. I carried the little diagram of who I am in Christ, and pulled it out a number of times before I shared with them. Each time, I was reminded of the resources I have inside me, and of the confidence God gives to those who see themselves the way He does. Not only did I get to share Christ with KISS that night, but God opened up doors for me to share with a number of other bands and athletes in the next few years, including the Beach Boys, Styx, Elton John, Olivia Newton John, John Denver, and a number of NBA basketball and major league baseball players. In other words, God not only gave me my personal mission in life, but the power to live it out. I am aware of what an ordinary person I am, but I'm also aware of what an extraordinary God we serve.

In a similar way, these "resources" inside of every new creature are there to accomplish something. Inside you, God put love, faith, power, spiritual gifts, etc. You don't need to beg for more! You have everything you need to fulfill your calling and influence others.

We each have the same number of muscles in our bodies, but we may not be able to demonstrate the same amount of strength. Why? It is because we have not taken the time to develop our muscles. In the same way, each Christian is as complete as every other believer, but we don't all demonstrate the same spiritual strength. Why? We have not developed our possessions! Review the diagram of possessions that God has given each of us. Which ones are strongly apparent in your life? Which do you need to embrace?

YOU HAVE NEW POTENTIAL

There is a third truth we learn from this text in 2 Corinthians 5:16-18. Being the new creatures He created, God wants us to step into a life of ministry. We all are supposed to have some kind of ministry, regardless of our occupation. Each of us is responsible to advance the Kingdom. Paul calls it the ministry of reconciliation. Verse 18 tells us that God has given us the ministry of reconciliation: "Now all these things are from God, who reconciled us to Himself through Christ, and gave us the ministry of reconciliation" (2 Corinthians 5:18).

Could you imagine a giant train engine pulling only one small car on a long journey? It would not be a good use of time and energy since the engine has much more potential than it is using. In the same way, it is foolish for us, as Christians, to use our great potential to only warm a pew on Sundays. We need to take people with us as we journey through this life to the gates of heaven. We have the potential to take a whole lot of other people with us to heaven.

There is a phenomenon among my family's pets. Otis, the cat, had been a part of my aunt and uncle's household for quite some time before Pierre came on the scene. Pierre, the puppy, was a little, perky toy poodle. Otis didn't know what to make of this new hyper playmate, so he tried to avoid him. But Pierre didn't have any other friends, so about two weeks into his stay, my relatives started noticing the dog was following the cat everywhere. Otis would jump on the couch, Pierre would jump on the couch. Otis would hop on the counter, Pierre would hop on the counter. Otis would climb a tree, and Pierre would climb a tree! My uncle was confused because, "dogs don't climb trees." Then it finally hit him; Pierre thought he was a cat! He had never known another dog before, so he assumed that he was just a younger version of Otis! That's the power of believing! That's the power of a strong sense of identity!

You have everything you need to fulfill your calling and influence others.

The Average Child...

I don't cause teachers trouble
My grades have been okay
I keep up on my chores at home
I'm in school everyday

My teachers think I'm average
My parents think so too
I wish I didn't know that
Cause there's things I'd like to do

I'd like to build a rocket ship
I've got a book that shows you how
Or start a stamp collection
Well, no use in trying now

'Cause, since I know I'm average
I'm just smart enough you see
To know there's nothing special
I should expect of me

I'm just part of that majority
That bumps part of the bell
Who live their lives unnoticed
In an average kind of hell.

That is *not* the way it has to be! Being a new creature and believing we are new creatures should dramatically change our lives.

Think about The Emancipation Proclamation. Abe Lincoln wrote it to free all of the slaves in the South. Yet, were all the slaves freed immediately after it was written? No, the Civil War continued for two more years. Even then, it wasn't until 100 years later, when the civil rights movement began, that this freedom started to become a reality. People had to stand up and say, "I am free and I will be free!" Likewise, we need to believe that we are free in Christ. Scripture is our emancipation proclamation. We need to stand up and claim our identity in Him.

STEPS FOR APPLICATION

1. Renew our perspective

When we sin, we begin to get extremely down on ourselves. After we have committed the same sin several times, we can assume God doesn't even want to hear from us anymore. We think that He is sick of hearing our confessions again and again. Instead, as a new creation, we should acknowledge our sin, thank Him for His forgiveness and begin to confess our new identity. It is not natural for our new nature to sin, but we still struggle with the flesh and our minds battle to go back to the old programming with which we have previously lived. However, we are not our old sinful selves—we are new creatures. We must think like new creatures.

2. Release our past

We must let go of our old patterns, sins, bad habits and relationships. This is the part that is often the hardest because it means letting go of what is familiar. Our identity cannot be attached to our past experience; it must be tied to our position in Christ. Our behavior must follow our belief. It might be helpful to make a list of your old patterns, habits and relationships. From these lifestyle ingredients, which ones are hindering your growth as a new creature? How will you strip them from your life? Will you also release them to God? Our worst sins arise as a result of our innate fear that we are nobody.

3. Remember our purpose

We must remember why God left us in this world! We must embrace His purpose for our lives if we're going to experience the power inside of us! Ultimately, God's purpose is for us to build the kingdom and advance the cause of Christ. This purpose is the most important business that we can be about. And we will never fully experience our identity in Christ and the fulfillment that comes from the realization of what we were created to do until we pursue this purpose. That doesn't mean that we have to drop all of our plans and start a church in Zimbabwe, but it does mean that we have to uncover and live out our God-given purpose — and realize how our purpose fits into God's great purpose for the whole world.

We need to stand up and claim our identity in Christ.

Our worst sins arise as a result of our innate fear that we are nobody.

ASSESS YOURSELF

Which of these three truths is most difficult to embrace? Why?

Which is making the biggest impact on you right now as a student? Why?

BRINGING IT ALL HOME

"In the end, our worst fears are not that we cannot do something significant. Our worst fears are that we might actually be someone and have something to offer that could change this world. This represents such a weight to us that we choose not to bear it, instead, living at a level far beneath our potential." –Nelson Mandela

EXERCISING SPIRITUAL DISCIPLINES

How You Can Stay Fit Through Spiritual Diet & Exercise

"Do you not know that in a race all the runners run, but only one gets the prize? Run in such a way as to get the prize. Everyone who competes in the games goes into strict training. They do it to get a crown that will not last; but we do it to get a crown that will last forever."
(1 Corinthians 9:24-25)

American Christians live with an irony. We've become obsessed with physical fitness. Therefore, we've bought into a myriad of physical fitness plans. We've also become obsessed with our spirituality ––yet most people do not buy into any kind of spiritual "fitness" plan; we are spiritually undisciplined. As George Barna says, "Americans are searching for God, but aren't willing to pay the price of admission."

My wife and I bought our first house in 1985. We purchased one in a subdivision where the builders put in the front lawn, but left the back lawn to be planted by the owner. It was just a big plot of dirt. Fortunately, they put a six-foot fence all the way around the backyard so no one could see the dirt. Thank God! That fence was my saving grace for almost three years. I did nothing to the backyard since no one could see it.

One day I stood at my sliding glass door looking out at the dirt. In that moment God and I had an unforgettable conversation. He impressed me with this truth: "Tim, you have treated your life like you have treated your lawn." Hmmm. I wasn't sure what that meant so I remained quiet and prayed, "Lord, what do you mean?"

Here is the truth God showed me that day. My front lawn looked great. It was the public side of my property. If you drove by my house you would have thought I had a green thumb. The shrubs, the palm trees, and the green grass all looked great. In the same way, the public side of my life was in great shape. I preached well. I dressed sharp. I had decent people skills. But like my back lawn, the private side of my life was dirt. I had given no time to my spiritual disciplines. And I kept an invisible fence up (just like on my property). No one could see that I failed to build any disciplines into my life. My private world was in shambles. Ouch!

"Americans are searching for God, but aren't willing to pay the price of admission."

George Barna

I remember making a decision that day—to commit that year to building spiritual disciplines back in my life, like I had in college. You see, once I graduated from college I thought I'd have more control of my calendar. Finally, I'd get my life back. Wrong. The pressure of work, marriage and mortgage payments became all consuming. So, God was forced to wait in line.

My hope is that this won't happen to you. I'm encouraging you to take time now to build a lifestyle of discipline—spiritual as well as physical—that you can take with you as long as you live. It's still another step you can take to live a life of influence.

THE ANALOGY OF MARRIAGE

Perhaps the best picture of what I'm challenging you to is the analogy of a marriage. Each of us understands that after every wedding comes a marriage. Note the analogy below:

1. **Conversion = The grace of a beautiful wedding.**
When we come to Christ, it's like a wedding; it's an event where we commit to a relationship.

2. **Spiritual Disciplines = The labor of a good, healthy marriage.**
Following our conversion, our relationship with God is only healthy as we invest effort into it.

REFLECT AND RESPOND

1. Are you sure you've had your spiritual wedding to Christ? Briefly describe your wedding in the space allotted below.

2. How is your marriage to Him? Is the relationship flourishing or merely surviving? Check one:

○ *Flourishing*   ○ *Maybe*   ○ *Not sure*   ○ *Merely surviving!*

Talk about which of the three groups of spiritual disciplines you are exercising the most.

WHAT ARE THE SPIRITUAL DISCIPLINES?

Richard Foster categorizes the spiritual disciplines into three groups. I offer definitions and Scripture for each of these at toward the end of this session:

THE INWARD DISCIPLINES...

>   Meditation   Prayer
>   Fasting   Study

THE OUTWARD DISCIPLINES...

>   Simplicity   Solitude
>   Submission   Service

THE CORPORATE DISCIPLINES...

>   Confession   Worship
>   Guidance   Celebration

Today, most of these are foreign to Christians in the Western world. Even the ones we do practice—such as prayer—are still minimized. Like so many failing marriages, 90% of Christians need to rescue their prayer lives from the tyranny of feelings. Spiritual disciplines do just that. They enable you to live on a higher level.

I know what you are thinking. The last thing you need is to add one more activity to your already busy schedule. I agree. Let me suggest, however, that this isn't what I am challenging you to do. Spiritual disciplines take no time—yet take all of our time, because they are meant to be part of an integrated life. It's not about adding some new activity to your agenda. Instead, I am talking about a whole new lifestyle where you think like God thinks and value what He values so you can act like He acts. We must start slow and small but eventually, we build a lifestyle.

Accomplished pianists or tennis players have built habits into their lives over years. They begin to operate from their subconscious mind. Discipline is second nature. For example, Venus Williams finds it harder to make a bad tennis shot than a good one. She must work at making a poor shot because she has trained herself to stroke the tennis ball the right way. Now, she doesn't have to think about the discipline of volleying on the tennis court. This is how spiritual disciplines are supposed to be. They become central to our lives and are integrated into our normal routine.

WHAT WOULD JESUS DO?

Jesus models the importance of spiritual disciplines in Mark 1:32-38. He interrupted His time with people to get time alone with His heavenly Father. He practiced the discipline of solitude and perhaps even the disciplines of prayer and meditation. He insisted on exercising these disciplines even in the face of great physical, spiritual and emotional needs. In fact, when He left the house one night, He left a crowded room of needy people. He had healed many of them, but not all of them. Peter led a search party to hunt Him down and bring Him back. However, Jesus did not allow the needs of people to determine His plans. He wouldn't let anything or anyone but God dictate His course.

OBSERVATIONS ON THE PASSAGE...

1. The pressure is on. The day was over but the public had just begun to make demands. (v.32)

2. The paradox is obvious. Jesus left in the middle of ministry time, with needs unmet. (v.35)

3. The point is clear. Jesus had to pause, leave the people and refuel His own life. (v.35)

4. The purpose is revealed. His Father renewed His perspective and gave Him direction. (v.38)

REFLECT AND RESPOND

Are you able to leave the needs and the clamor of people to refuel your life? Circle one:

Yes, I do so regularly   **Most of the time**   **Sometime**   **Rarely**

List some of the things that strike you most about Jesus' interaction with Peter and the disciples.

1.

2.

3.

LIVING THE FASTED LIFE

In Matthew 17:14-21, Jesus brings up another spiritual discipline, fasting. It seems to be a source of spiritual strength against the enemy. Jesus explained to His disciples that some people aren't delivered from demonic forces except through the discipline of fasting. Interesting. Did you ever notice, however, Jesus didn't have to run and begin fasting in order to cast the demon out? He was living a life of spiritual discipline—a fasted life. He was prepared to meet the enemy daily.

OBSERVATIONS ON THE PASSAGE...

1. The disciples were unable to meet a need that Jesus fully expected them to meet (v.16-17).

2. Jesus privately explained that disciplines like prayer and fasting are often necessary, when confronting the enemy (v.21).

3. Jesus didn't have to retreat to pray and fast in this case. He was living the fasted life (v.18).

> *"I am fasting from the last word."*
> - Dallas Willard

Fasting isn't just about avoiding food. You can fast from any fleshly or material pleasure that you believe might be preventing you from hearing God's voice or maintaining a Spirit-led life. I recommend you examine your life and determine what's keeping you from living this kind of life. It may be food, it may be TV, it may be listening to too much music. I remember hearing a story about Dallas Willard, a wonderful author on the subject of spiritual disciplines. He was doing a lecture in which he fielded questions from the audience afterward. One man raised his hand and began to comment on Willard's lecture. This man got completely off track and began to contradict what Dallas Willard had said. Instead of correcting him, Willard just politely acknowledged his comments and went on to the next question.

Later, Dallas Willard's team asked him about it backstage. "Why didn't you correct that guy in the audience?" they asked.

Dallas Willard smiled. "Because today," he replied, "I am fasting from having the last word." He went on to explain that he was prone to want to always get the last word in when he was engaged in an argument or conversation. He concluded that he needed to "fast" from allowing himself to get the last word. Hmmm. Sounds like something I need to do.

REFLECT AND RESPOND

When adversity overtakes you as a student, how do you respond? Are you calm and ready to face it? Which of the options below reflects your lifestyle? Check all which apply.

- ○ I face it calmly
- ○ Sometimes I am forced to face it
- ○ I usually face it
- ○ Rarely do I face it

Are you living a "fasted life"? Jot down one or two ways are you practicing spiritual disciplines as a student.

THE PURPOSE OF SPIRITUAL DISCIPLINES

Discipline is like a bridge that takes you from where you are to where you want to be. Spiritual disciplines are not meant to be a drag. They are a friend, not a foe. In fact, when you live a life of discipline you'll find you have the freedom and the power to live the life you really want to live. King Solomon once said, "One who hates correction is stupid" (Proverbs 12:1). When you are disciplined you like yourself more. When you aren't—you can actually lose respect for yourself.

If you are practicing them effectively the spiritual disciplines will restore God's…

> **PERSPECTIVE** (Balanced, "big picture" thinking)
> **POWER** (Resources and refreshment for the day)
> **PURPOSE** (A sense His mission and call on your life)
> **PEACE** (Poise and inner-tranquility, even in outer turmoil)
> **PRESENCE** (Experience of intimacy with Him)

These words are supposed to describe the normal Christian life. Isn't it interesting that we usually think a person is extraordinary if they exhibit the qualities above? God's desire is for spiritual disciplines to enhance your relationship to Him. They are not an end in themselves. They are like the rules for a game. For instance, the game of soccer has rules. The rules are not the game itself—they only help players play the game well. Spiritual disciplines help you do your relationship with God very well. They provide a platform for intimacy with Him.

GOD'S DESIGN FOR YOUR LIFE

The Bible teaches that we are three-fold beings: spirit, soul and body (I Thessalonians 5:23). We are spirit beings (like God), who have a soul, and who live in a body.

Your spirit was originally designed by God to be in a dominant position. It is the part of your heart that connects you with God. Paul wrote, "The Spirit Himself testifies together with our spirit that we are God's children" (Romans 8:16). Jesus said, "God is Spirit, and they that worship Him must worship in spirit and in truth (John 4:24)."

Your soul, strictly defined, is your personality. The original Greek word used in the New Testament is the word psuche. It is where we get our word, psyche. It literally represents your mind, your will and your emotions. Your personality isn't bad, but it was designed to play a subordinate

Which of the 12 spiritual disciplines do you practice most consistently? Describe how it helps you.

role to your spirit. Your mind, will and emotions all can find a way to express themselves, but only in step with your spirit that is connected with God's Spirit. That's why Jesus said He only did what His heavenly Father bid Him to do. He had a strong mind; He debated the Pharisees and beat them! He had a strong will; He took a whip to the money-changers in the Temple. He had strong emotions; He wept when Lazarus died. Yet, all of these expressions of His personality were screened by the Spirit. What came out was obedience to God.

Take a moment and study the diagram below. In it, I attempt to describe how your inner-self was designed to operate. Notice your spirit is on top. It is dominant. Your soul (made up of your mind, will and emotions) is subordinate to your spirit. When your mind, will or emotions wants to express themselves, that expression should come up and be screened by the spirit, which is taking directions from the Holy Spirit. What comes out is acceptable service to God (Romans 12:2).

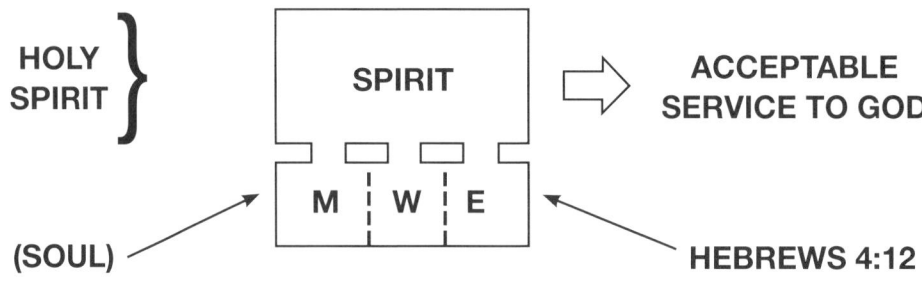

WHAT HAPPENED TO US?

In the Garden of Eden, Adam and Eve were created with a spirit, soul and body. They enjoyed unbroken intimacy with God. However, when they sinned they usurped their personality apart from God's leading. That's what sin is. It's you leading the way instead of God. In Eve's case, Satan attacked her mind and emotions, "Did God really say you cannot eat this fruit?" And did He say, "If you eat it, you'll be like God." In Adam's case Satan attacked his will. Adam knew better than to eat that fruit. God had specifically told him not to eat from that tree. In both of their cases, however, Satan attacked their soul. Suddenly, their soul took a dominant position over their spirit. They had broken fellowship with God. They now led with their own power, not God's. This problem still continues today.

How do we return our spirit to a dominant position? How do we know when it is God leading us and not our own thoughts? How do we know a decision is His will and not our will? The answer has everything to do with spiritual disciplines.

THE ROLE OF GOD'S WORD

Take a fresh look at Hebrews 4:12. In this passage we read that the Word of God is the only instrument God has given us, which discerns our thoughts and intentions. Further, we read that it divides our soul and our spirit.

"For the Word of God is living and effective and sharper than any two-edged sword, penetrating as far as to divide soul, spirit, joints, and marrow, it is a judge of the ideas and thoughts of the heart" (Hebrews 4:12).

When you practice the spiritual discipline of studying God's Word, you not only feed your spirit and renew your mind, but you place your spirit in a dominant position. As you consistently feed yourself with Scripture you maintain a dominant spirit. You enable yourself to hear God's voice, think like He thinks, value what He values and act like He acts. It would be difficult to overestimate the importance of the Word of God in our lives.

FOCUS: THE DISCIPLINE OF SOLITUDE AND STUDY

In the final portion of this chapter we won't take time to examine every spiritual discipline. However, we will focus on one of them as a case study. The discipline of Scripture study is intended to enable you to think Biblically, to think like God thinks. The following are suggestions on how you might develop this discipline while practicing the principle of solitude.

Make an appointment.
Decide on a time and a place to get alone with God. You must schedule it just as you do other "important" meetings. If Jesus did this, how much more do we need to? Choose a period of time and a place that best enables you to get trouble-free blocks of time, consistently.

Begin by becoming quiet. Then, ask God to speak specifically to you.
Hearing God's voice is no accident. He speaks to us regularly, but we are not always listening. Remember young Samuel learning to hear God's

voice in I Samuel 3:1-10? Samuel shows us that God speaks to those who get into position to hear His voice by becoming quiet and still, and who are obedient to what He has to say.

Bring the right resources with you.
I believe the best times of meditation and personal study come when I have my Study Bible, a journal, a pen and sometimes an extra commentary or devotional guide as well. So many of these resources are available online at sites like YouVersion.com and BibleGateway.com that all you may need is your laptop! Whichever route you decide, don't understimate the importance of having the right tools available. Don't be afraid to trade off and try new resources to keep your interaction fresh.

Develop a game plan for study.
Don't consistently approach the Bible and just flip it open to whatever passage comes up, like some magic book. You must prepare for meaningful conversation with God, just like you do with a person you love. You don't just barge in the door, run up to them and begin asking for things. Compare your life to running down a hill. It takes a few steps just to slow down, once you've decided to stop! Deep conversations often require a "slowing down time". Perhaps you can start by reading a Psalm – then ask God to speak to you. Next, predetermine the chapter or book you will focus on for the week. Your goal should be to get the whole counsel of God, so plan to read through entire books of the Bible, even if you do so a little at a time. Your game plan can come from a devotional book if that's more comfortable.

Determine to read until you get a principle or truth you can practice.
Most of us still read for "information" rather than "application." D. L. Moody reminded us that "God's word was not written to inform us but to transform us." Keep reading the Scripture until you sense God is sharing something with you, personally. Read until you "get something." Discover the adventure of studying until you find something that you've never tried to obey before, then go and find a "laboratory" in which to experiment.

Write out what God is saying through His Word.
Whether or not you feel you are a "writer," this is a solid discipline. Writing not only keeps your mind on track, but it I gives you a record of what

"God's Word was not written to inform us but to transform us."
- D.L. Moody

God is teaching you from week to week. It will also act as an accountability partner for you as you will be less apt to buy into some heretical belief when you are writing things down.

A MODEL FOR STUDY

I begin by reading a portion of Scripture. Then, I take my notebook (journal) and write out three brief paragraphs on what I've read. Because I'm not into journaling, I just "jot" a few sentences in response to three questions below.

Date: _____

Text: _____

ONE TIME - What was God saying at one time to the original audience?

ALL TIME - What is the all-time, universal truth I can learn from this?

NOW TIME - What is the application I can make today?

I remember the first Scripture on which I practiced this discipline. It was Luke 20:26-47.

ONE TIME - My first paragraph on what God was saying to the original audience was simple. I paraphrased how the scribes tried to trap Jesus by asking Him a trick question: Should we pay taxes to Caesar? If He said yes, He would be submitting to Caesar's lordship; if He said no, He'd be rebelling against the law, and could be arrested. Jesus answered the question with a question, "Whose image is on the coin?" When they replied, "Caesars," Jesus responded, "Then render unto Caesar what is Caesar's, but render to God what is God's." And no one dared asked Him anything else.

ALL TIME - My second paragraph was illuminating. When I asked myself what the universal principle was from this text I suddenly saw that Jesus was teaching a principle from His question. Whenever an object has an image stamped on it, then that object belongs to the one whose image is on it. The coin had Caesar's image on it. Therefore they should surrender to Caesar. Those people, however, were made in God's image and should be surrendering themselves to God! This passage became a great lesson in surrender and ownership.

NOW TIME - Suddenly my personal application was clear. I began to journal what portions of my life I still needed to surrender to Jesus' Lordship. It was like a light bulb went off inside of me. My study time became very personal and poignant. It was life changing. And to think, I wouldn't have even seen this principle had I not forced myself to really study and journal the Scripture.

Learn to meditate on the specific word God has for you.
Once you've read the text and written out its specific meaning and application for you, GO BACK and meditate on (even memorize) the specific verse(s) that God is using to speak to you. This is the practice that will allow the Holy Spirit to say several things to you… from a single passage! Note the difference between Eastern and Biblical meditation:

Eastern Meditation: The emptying of oneself; it is an escape from the misery of this world's existence. Detachment is the final goal of Eastern meditation.

Biblical Meditation: The filling of oneself with God through His truth. It is the reflection on His Word changing us from the inside out. Attachment is the final goal of this Biblical meditation.

Meditation Can Include the Following Exercises:

➢ **IMAGINATION**: Visually picture the action of the text in your mind; try to imagine yourself in the movement of the text.

➢ **ISOLATION**: Concentrate on one key word in what you have read and let it mull over in your mind again and again. Study a Bible dictionary to gain its deeper meaning. If you do not have one, you may find one in the church library you can use. If not, go buy one! They are usually cheaper than an English textbook.

➢ **INVOCATION**: Invoke God to make it so in your life; pray the Scriptures that they will become your autobiography.

➢ **MEMORIZATION**: Commit a meaningful portion of the text to memory. Focus on these words until you can personalize them for yourself.

➢ **AFFIRMATION**: Affirm that these words be so in your life and thoughts.

Key Principle: Each Scripture has but one interpretation, but many applications. (II Peter 1:19-21; James 1:22)

INTERNALIZE THE WORD THROUGH OBEDIENCE.

While Scripture memorization may be easy or difficult for you, there is one sure-fire way to internalize the Bible. It isn't memorization cards with verses on them or even setting the Scripture to music (although both of these help)! It is a three-fold practice from the Bible itself, found in Ezra 7:10: Study it, practice it, and share it.

A SUMMARY OF THE SPIRITUAL DISCIPLINES

1. Meditation (Psalm 119:78)
The focus which enables us to hear God's voice and obey His Word

2. Prayer (Matthew 6:5-15)
The interactive conversation with God about what we are doing together

3. Fasting (Matthew 6:16-18)
The voluntary denial of an otherwise normal function for the sake of intense spiritual activity

4. Study (II Timothy 2:15)
The process where the mind explores truth, allowing it to penetrate and adjust our perspective

5. Simplicity (Matthew 6:22-24)
An inward removal of clutter that results in a lifestyle of being focused instead of scattered

6. Solitude (Mark 6:31)
The creation of open, empty space where we are freed from competing loyalties and seek God

7. Submission (Ephesians 5:21)
The discipline which allows us to let go of the need to control and the burden of needing to get our own way

8. Service (John 13:1-16)
The many little deaths of looking and giving beyond ourselves

9. **Worship (John 4:23)**

The expression of adoration and awe toward God, resulting in the experience His glory

10. **Guidance (Acts 15:28)**

The experience of knowing in our lives an interactive friendship with God

11. **Confession (James 5:16)**

To express agreement with God over your condition and experience healing from past stains, chains and pains

12. **Celebration (Philippians 4:4)**

The expression of joy which results from reflecting on God's character and conduct toward us

YOUR PRACTICE OF THE SPIRITUAL DISCIPLINES

As you engage yourself in the practice of spiritual disciplines, focus on one at a time. As you begin to build them into your life keep the following parable in mind.

I remember hearing about a man who decided to purchase a very expensive vase for his living room. It took him quite a while to make up his mind to buy it but once he did he was so excited to take it home and find the perfect spot for it in his home.

Upon arriving at home he determined to put it on the mantle of his fireplace, a very visible place in the living room. It was gorgeous. Every day he'd look at it and marvel at its beauty.

However, after a week he began to feel that something was wrong. The vase was so regal that it almost seemed out of place in that living room. After all, the curtains were old and shabby. After careful thought he drew his conclusion. He would upgrade his curtains. He couldn't allow them to stay in the same room as that nice, new vase.

Soon he began to notice the same thing about the sofa and his easy chair. They just didn't fit with the vase or the new curtains. So he went out and bought a new sofa and chair. Next, it was the rug and the coffee table that just didn't fit the room. They got upgraded, too. Within a matter of months the whole room was transformed.

"Each Scripture has but one interpretation, but many applications."

This little parable is an analogy of what ought to happen when Jesus Christ takes His rightful spot in our lives. Through spiritual disciplines we allow Him to be front and center, and we suddenly see how each part of our life needs to be changed. Disciplines enable us to make those changes permanent and furnish us with a life that is fitting for the Master. Here's to a disciplined life of influence for the rest of your life.

ASSESSMENT

Which of the disciplines do you already have in place in your life as a student? List them in any order in this space.

Which ones do you still need to incorporate more fully into your life? List them as well.

APPLICATION

What discipline will you invest yourself in first? Choose one and jot it down here!

Describe if you can what will be your first step to incorporate this discipline in your life!

PLAYING TO YOUR STRENGTHS
Finding Your Zone to Make the Biggest Splash You Can

"A gift opens doors for a man and brings him before the great."
(Proverbs 18:16)

If you saw the movie, "The Blind Side" starring Sandra Bullock, you are familiar with the story of Michael Oher. He came from a difficult background. With a father in prison and a mother addicted to drugs, Michael spent much of his youth in foster homes and eventually ended up homeless. Luckily, he was taken in by the Tuohy family and finally had a place to call home. He began to play football because of his size but struggled to play well until one day when everything changed.

There's a great scene in the movie where Leigh Anne Tuohy (portrayed by Sandra Bullock), is watching Michael's football practice. Although he towers over the other players, he's just average at his position. She explains to Michael that the team is like his family. She wants him to protect his teammates just like he had protected her and his little brother. Leigh Anne recognized his strength and drew it out of him.

This small change in perspective sparks a fire in Michael and he unleashes a powerful hit on the next play. Once he recognized what was inside, his true colors came out—and shown brightly. Finding his real strength moved him from "good" to "great." Michael Oher went on to be a first round draft pick in the NFL and continues to play professional football today.

This is the move I want to help you make in your life. It's a move from merely involving yourself to investing yourself in something. It means investing your life in a role where you truly fit. It's a shift from just drawing a paycheck at work to diving into work you feel you were built to do. It may be your job, it may be a volunteer position, or it may be something you do on the side—but it's finding a work to do that wakes you up in the morning. It's a matter of finding your strength. I like to call it your "zone."

What is your "zone?" It is where you make the biggest splash. Where you are strong. Most people don't find it until midlife; some never find it. They trudge along in a mediocre life, with no passion, and without anything

Ben Franklin called wasted strengths "sundials in the shade."

they feel they should give their life to. The word "mediocre" is an interesting word that describes this life. It used to be a term used by mountain climbers or rock climbers. Mediocre literally means: "middle of the rock." It described people who lost their zest for finishing the climb and stopped halfway up the mountain. Whenever you aren't in your strength zone, you'll be tempted to stop short. Logic dilutes the zeal you once had, and you rationalize why it's best to stop short of excellence. You become average…or mediocre at that activity. The tragedy of life is not that each of us doesn't have enough strengths; it's that we fail to use the ones we have. Ben Franklin called wasted strengths "sundials in the shade."

REFLECT AND RESPOND
What would you say are your top two strengths? List them below.

1.

2.

PLAYING TO YOUR STRENGTHS OR WORKING ON YOUR WEAKNESSES?

I call this chapter "Playing to Your Strengths." But just what is a strength? According to authors Marcus Buckingham and Donald Clifton, a strength is a "consistent near-perfect performance in an activity." This happens when you consistently excel at something while others say it looks like you did it with little effort. Can you excel at something that is not your strength? I suppose so. But it will sap you and you cannot do it for long. Playing outside of your "zone" for long periods of time is both difficult and draining.

We generally drift toward something that requires less effort. We take the path of least resistance and the path of least persistence. However, outside our "zone" we won't excel. We'll likely become average. Now, here's the clincher: people don't pay for average. Nobody says, "Hey, let's go out tonight. Let's go to an average restaurant, take in an average movie, and end the evening with some average coffee and dessert." Why? Because we want to experience excellence. We pay for strengths.

Unfortunately, common sense says that if you have a strength and a weakness, you should spend time working on your weakness. After all,

---

Group Up
How do you discover your strengths?

People don't pay for average.

we generally want to be well-rounded adults, don't we? No one wants to be weak in anything, do they? We want to be viewed as Renaissance men and women!

The fact of the matter is, we have it backwards. You will always have some weaknesses. Some of history's greatest leaders had obvious weaknesses. They became great because they focused on their strengths. I am encouraging you to find and focus on your strengths.

Let's play a little game to explain why this is so strategic. Suppose you have a strength and a weakness. On a scale of 1 to 10, let's say your weakness is a "3" and your strength is an "8." Because our normal tendency is to work on our weaknesses, we spend lots of time trying to get strong in that area. However, a weakness rarely becomes a strong suit. With lots of work, a "3" may only become a "5." We seldom get a weakness beyond average. And people don't pay for average. However, if you work on what you are good at, an "8" may become a "10." You become excellent. People do notice and pay for excellence. Effective leaders play to their strengths and manage around their weaknesses.

WHAT MAKES UP A STRENGTH?

If a strength is a consistent, near-perfect performance in an activity, then what enables us to pull that off? What makes up a strength? Let me suggest four ingredients:

1. Natural Talents – the abilities you naturally possess

Perhaps you've always been good at organizing things or singing or graphic design. Talents are naturally occurring patterns of thought, feeling or behavior. Most of us have themes of talent. They are abilities you have even before you become a Christian. Atheists can have great God-given talents. Talents become strengths when we groom them over time, through practice and evaluation. They can surface at different parts of our life, but often you feel you've always liked or been good at them.

2. Knowledge – the insight you have on a subject

In a strength area you have a natural curiosity and understanding. Knowledge consists of the facts and lessons learned in that area. When you have it, people may seek you out to discover information on that area. You have insight on it. This insight involves both nature and nurture. You may feel you've always had insight on a subject and you have a curiosity to discover more about it. Maybe you have a keen insight about mechanical things or about how to communicate a principle or how to connect with people in relationships. Knowledge means you know a lot about it and want to know more.

3. Spiritual gifts – the divine enabling you have to serve others
Spiritual gifts are abilities you gain after you become a Christian. God imparts them to you through the Holy Spirit. The Bible teaches that every believer has at least one spiritual gift (1 Peter 4:10, 1 Corinthians 12:4-7). I believe most of us have a spiritual gift-mix: a mixture or set of gifts from God that we can use to advance His Kingdom on the earth. Spiritual gifts are to be used for spiritual ministry. (God did not give you spiritual gifts to increase the profits of Google.) These gifts are listed in the New Testament in places like 1 Corinthians 12, Ephesians 4:10-11, 1 Peter 4:7-11 and Romans 12. I believe all of us have one of the "motivational gifts" listed in Romans 12:4-8.

4. Acquired skills – the aptitude you gain to take steps in an activity
Over time, you may have picked up some skills that you've been able to add to your arsenal. Skills are the steps you choose to take in an activity. Your strength may involve a set of skills. Because a strength area involves a curiosity to know more, you generally acquire a greater aptitude in that area and know the steps to take to get something done. Generally, a strength begins with a talent. Knowledge is added along the way. Eventually, these lead to acquired skills—a set of aptitudes you accumulate to help you get a job done. All of these together make up a primary strength.

Let me illustrate how these ingredients can play out in someone's life. To be drawn toward strangers and to enjoy the challenge of connecting with them is a talent. Let's say a person with this talent becomes a salesman. To make this a strength he must also learn how to describe his product's unique features, which is knowledge. In addition, he should learn how to ask open-ended questions to understand the prospect's needs, which is a skill. A person could become a strong salesperson by combining these ingredients in a career. I believe, however, for some activity to truly become a strength, a person must begin with a talent or a spiritual gift. This is a God-given enabling that allows you to combine nature and nurture.

You possess the raw material and later develop that ability to its fullest.

One of my primary strengths is teaching. Today, I love to equip others to live a life of purpose and influence. I hope that becomes clear as you read this book. This predisposition to teach covers all four ingredients above. Before I became a Christian it took the form of enjoying writing projects in school. I'd dig out some obscure information for a paper and enjoy sharing it with my history class (natural talent). I had a curiosity to find out more about certain subjects and how to communicate them in a creative way (knowledge). Later, when I met Christ, I found I wanted to teach and equip people for ministry. (That isn't to say it's wrong to teach outside of a Christian context. I just had a keen interest in doing it to help students become influential for God's Kingdom). My teaching role became one I used in the body of Christ (spiritual gift). Finally, I found over time that I was discovering new ways to share truths with others. I not only discovered new things to teach but new ways to teach them (acquired skills).

Acquired skill is a God-given enabling that allows you to combine nature and nurture.

REFLECT AND RESPOND

Based on the four elements that make up a strength, list one or more in each element you have discovered in your life.

Natural talents

Knowledge

Spiritual gifts

Acquired skills

GOD'S NATURE

Let me give a disclaimer. Finding your strengths doesn't mean that God is bound to use them in this manner all the time. You will find times He will break you and actually use a weakness or a broken place in your life for His glory. He may receive more glory in using your weakness because everyone can see it wasn't you that accomplished the result; it was Him. Do you remember the story of Gideon in Judges 6-7? Do you remember Moses in Exodus 4-6? God took a broken place or a weakness in those men and turned it around. However, God—Creator of all the gifts in the universe—generally places gifts and passions inside of you to use them. He wants to capitalize on the strengths you have.

This was never more clear than when Jesus told the parable of the Talents in Matthew 25. In the story, a landowner gives a set of talents to three servants. To the first, He gave five talents. To the second, He gave two and to the third, He gave one. He told them to "occupy" until He returned for them. When the Owner returned, He found the first servant had multiplied his talents; the five had become ten. The Owner affirmed the servant's return on investment. Next, the Owner discovered the second servant had also doubled his talents. Once again, the Owner was pleased. Unfortunately, this Owner found the third servant idle. He had only buried the talent. When the Owner returned, the servant dug it up, blew the dirt off and gave it back to his Master. At this point the story becomes very interesting. The Owner (who represents God) gets very angry at the third servant for not multiplying his single talent. In fact, you never see God get more angry with anyone—not prostitutes, not murderers, not thieves—than He does with His own servant who did nothing with what he had been given. Wow. What's most intriguing to me about the story is this: the third servant didn't lose his talent; he just didn't use it. Hmmm. I think God is serious about us using what we possess for His Kingdom.

REFLECT AND RESPOND

Do you have any buried talents?

Yes   No   Maybe   Don't know

Are there any God-given strengths you have set on the shelf indefinitely that you know God wants to use?

Yes   No   Maybe   Don't know

If the answer is "yes," what do you think you should do about it? What is one step you could take to use your talent for God?

HOW DO WE KNOW WE ARE IN OUR ZONE?

Once you are aware of this issue of strengths, you'll find there are symptoms attached to working in the area of your strengths. You'll know you are playing in your zone. How do we know we are in our zone? Consider the following symptoms:

1. In your zone, you are most <u>intuitive</u>. You'll have a natural intuition about that arena that others lack. You seem to know what to do to get results.

2. In your zone, you are most <u>productive</u>. You will bear more fruit and get more accomplished in this area than you do in other areas.

3. In your zone, you are most <u>comfortable</u>. You'll feel at home working in this arena more than others; in fact, you'll be tempted to want to do nothing else.

4. In your zone, you are most <u>satisfied</u>. You'll not only feel comfortable, you'll sense deep fulfillment. You might even sense: this is what I was built to do!

5. In your zone, you are most <u>influential</u>. In your strength area, you will have more influence and may be called upon to offer leadership in that arena.

6. In your zone, you are most <u>confident</u>. Even if you are not a confident person, in the area of your strength, you'll feel more confident than other areas of life.

Consider this story. Jimmy was a strange little kid growing up. His parents noticed early on he didn't become mesmerized with sports like the other boys in the neighborhood. In fact, he didn't like most of the normal things that boys like. Instead, he had a strange fixation with socks. You read it right. Jimmy liked to play with the socks in his drawer at home. He would pull them out and make them talk; he'd give them certain voices and personalities. At first, his parents thought he was just weird. They'd never seen any child play with their socks before. Thank God, they understood this idea of helping their children play to their strengths. They fostered his

Group Up
Which of the six strength zones can you identify in your own life?

creative disposition and bought him all colors and sizes. They let him play with socks, instead of playing with the other kids outside…and boy am I glad they did. I have enjoyed what little Jimmy made of this obsession. As an adult, Jim Henson made a living out of his fixation—and called them: Muppets.

REFLECT AND RESPOND

Think about the previous statements. Have you participated in an activity where you felt very comfortable, confident, productive and intuitive about it? Jot it down in this space.

Are there any patterns about the kind of activities you feel best about?

DEEPENING YOUR INFLUENCE

Everyone has something we all need. The key is to find that something and make it a strength. Make it something others will recognize as your contribution to them, and to the world around you. To live a life of influence, I believe you must discover and develop a strength in your life. You may have a little influence because of your character or your personality, but zeroing in on your "zone" and playing to your strengths will expand that influence. From a human standpoint, real influence comes from your character, your personality and your strengths. Once you find your strength and play in your zone—you will increase the influence you have with others.

During the 1990s, Michael Jordan became one of the greatest basketball players in the game. Some would say he's the greatest of all time. He led the Chicago Bulls to three championships, before he retired from the game. Michael packed out the United Center every game. People came out to watch his gift in action. Based on his large gift, he became a major influence in the world. He began doing commercials for loads of products. Even after his last retirement from management for the Washington Wizards, he was still doing advertisements for batteries and underwear! What does he know about batteries or underwear, you ask? Nothing more than you or me…but he's doing commercials because his gift gave him great influence.

During his first retirement, he did something extraordinary. He went on to play minor league baseball. Was that his gift zone? Absolutely not. He was not even mediocre as a baseball player. After just one season, he returned to the game of basketball. He was back in his zone. He won three more championships in a row. His gift deepened his influence again. While Michael's gift is a bit of an exaggeration, he still illustrates the point of this chapter. His gift gave him his influence. So will yours.

Proverbs 18:16 tells us: "A gift opens doors for a man and brings him before the great." This is another way of saying your gift provides you with influence. But, there's another benefit of finding your strength and using your gift. Your strength will resource the goals you set in your life. It's likely to pay for what you want to accomplish.

While I was in college I took on my first paid leadership position. I became a youth pastor. I dreamed of creating a multimedia presentation to take into the public high schools in my area. After putting the plan on paper, I realized it was going to cost thousands of dollars. As a college student, I had no discretionary money. One night, I sat in my dorm room, whining to God that I didn't have the money to do this project.

While I was praying, God impressed me with this profound truth. It was as though He said to me: "I have already given you every resource you need to do what I have called you to do." Hmmm. I didn't understand this at first because I understood "resource" to mean money—and I didn't have any money. Confused, I asked God what He was saying to me. He didn't speak in an audible voice, but during that prayer time He reminded me that I was a commercial art major in college. I had a portfolio of cartoons that I had drawn for the university newspaper. God reminded me that He gave me that gift, and I was to use it to fund the multimedia project.

To make a long story short, I set out the next Monday morning, in a suit and tie, with my portfolio of cartoons under my arm. I approached the editors of four local newspapers in the surrounding area, and proposed a deal. I would do editorial cartoons for them on local and state issues—for $10 a cartoon. (At the time they were purchasing editorial cartoons from national syndicates, on national issues). All four editors said yes. By the next week, I had more newspapers take me up on my deal. I had my own

"A gift opens doors for a man and brings him before the great" (Proverbs 18:16).

little syndicate going, and within two semesters, I had more than enough money to pay for the equipment I needed. My God-given gift funded my ministry.

REFLECT AND RESPOND
Briefly share with someone else a time when your gifts gave you influence. Describe it to them as part of the outpouring of your gift.

Have your gifts ever helped you reach a goal? Describe when and how!

MINISTRY VS. MARKETPLACE
One big source of guilt for many Christian students is not being called into "full-time ministry." Obviously, some students are called into vocational ministry, but most are not. Those who enter the marketplace often feel like "second-class citizens" or like players on the "B" team rather than the "A" team. After all, aren't pastors or missionaries more spiritual? Doesn't God smile on them a bit more than those of us who work in corporate America?

Let me say something for the record. Those who enter the marketplace often have a greater opportunity to minister to those who don't know Christ than pastors do. Your credibility will come from your character, your personality and your gift. Develop them and celebrate the role where God has placed you.

There are two ways you can look at the marketplace:

Marketplace as a mission. Some enter the workforce and see their job as a place to live out their personal mission statement. They don't wait

Those who enter the marketplace often have a greater opportunity to minister to those who don't know Christ than pastors do.

until they go to church and can serve as a volunteer in some ministry there. They are in their mission all day.

Marketplace as a source of funds for mission. Others view the corporate world as a place they can make money in order to fund ministry projects, local churches and missionaries overseas. They see their gift at making money as a way to underwrite the causes they believe in.

There is a story of one young missionary candidate was confused about this subject. He married his sweetheart, and the two of them interviewed at a missions agency, to be placed in an unreached tribe on a foreign field. In that interview, he committed he would work hard, share Christ with as many people as possible, and be a good steward of the resources God had given him.

Just months after arriving on the mission field, tragedy struck. This young man's wife realized she was not cut out for life on the mission field. They would have to return home for her to survive. This was devastating to him. On one hand, he felt called to be married to his bride, but on the other, he felt called to impact the world for Christ. Now he felt torn between the two. Laying in bed one night he wrestled with God in prayer. Suddenly, a light went off in his head. God reminded him he could keep his original commitment to work hard, to share Christ with as many people as possible and to be a good steward of the resources God had given him. With great resolve he decided he would go to work for his dad and keep that promise at home, in New York. His dad was a dentist who had started a little business on the side. He was producing unfermented wine for local church communion services. He asked his dad if he could take over that little business and build it into an enterprise that could bless the world for Christ. And he did. My guess is you have consumed some of this man's grape juice. His name is Charles Welch, and he built one of the largest juice companies in the country. Mr. Welch has given hundreds of thousands of dollars away to the cause of world missions. In fact, he did more for the cause of missions not going, than he would have if he had gone overseas. Staying in the marketplace and funding the mission was a greater gift for him. The fact of the matter is, missionaries don't have to cross the sea—they just have to see the cross.

Mr. Welch committed to work hard, share Christ, and be a good steward of his resources.

REFLECT AND RESPOND

How do you view your career as you develop it during college? Do you see it as your mission or as your way to fund your mission? (Neither view is wrong. The apostle Paul called himself a "tentmaker." He made tents to pay for his ministry in Asia. At other times he was in ministry full time).

Think about a way to combine your mission with your job. Jot your ideas in the space below.

YOUR SPIRITUAL GIFTS

Before we discuss a plan to discover your strengths, let me take a minute and talk over your spiritual gifts. If you have invited Christ to take over your life, you have the Holy Spirit living in you (John 14). The Holy Spirit brought with Him at least one spiritual gift and placed it inside of you. It is likely you have a set of spiritual gifts. These gifts are meant to be used as you serve the body of Christ and the world around you. Check out these statements about gifts in the Bible.

An Overview of Spiritual Gifts

1. **The New Testament lists at least twenty-five gifts of the Spirit.**
   Different churches vary in their view of which gifts are in operation today. But the fact is, you have some inside of you to be used to serve others.

2. **Each Christian has a primary motivational gift.**
   The list of gifts in Romans 12 is key. They are frequently called "motivational gifts." I see these gifts as the "hub of the wheel" around which your other gifts revolve.

3. **The Holy Spirit wants to reveal a supernatural Jesus through your gifts.**
   When you use your gifts in a mature way they demonstrate Jesus to others. They are designed to reveal a supernatural Jesus, exhibiting to people you have Christ inside.

4. **Like muscles, your gifts can be present but undeveloped.**
   Just because you don't see the gift in operation doesn't mean it's not there. Some people have muscles inside that are not developed—just like spiritual gifts.

5. **Gifts work like assignments or positions on a team.**
   In a football game, each player has a position to play, where they are strong. If a ball is fumbled, however, a defensive tackle doesn't avoid it because it's not his normal job to carry footballs. He knows the goal is to get to the end zone, even though he normally plays a defensive position.

6. **God's primary purpose for spiritual gifts is to advance His kingdom.**
   Your heavenly Father's purpose is not to raise your self-esteem by using them. It is to advance His rule and reign on the earth.

Spiritual gifts are meant to be used in ministry by mature Christians who not only experience the gifts of the Spirit but also the fruit of the Spirit. This maturity enables us to be used frequently in one primary way. Yet, we can enjoy being called upon outside of our gift zone once in a while when necessary. For instance, if you were to see a horrible car accident take place right outside your dorm or apartment, you wouldn't run out there and explain that you cannot help because you are not a doctor! That's ridiculous. You would call the doctor, but you would also serve that victim in whatever way you could until the doctor arrived. This is a picture of spiritual gifts. Sometimes we must serve a need outside of our gifts; however, by and large, God wants to use us in our gift area.

Sadly, this is not the norm in the body of Christ. Most believers still do not serve in their gift area. In fact, the Church generally suffers from "The Football Problem." Let me describe it to you. Every football game has two components: first, there are 22 people on the field in desperate need of rest. Second, there are 50,000 people in the stands in desperate need of exercise! Ouch. What a picture of most churches. A handful of people doing all the work; the rest of us sitting around watching all the action. We must reverse this reality wherever we go.

Group Up
What prevents people from using their gifts?

WHAT HAPPENS IF WE DON'T USE OUR GIFTS?

In 1 Peter 4:7-11, we are encouraged to use our gifts to serve others. In fact, it's a command. From these verses we learn three primary truths about gifts. If you don't step out and use your special gift…

1. **You rob yourself of being in God's will. (v. 10)**

2. **You rob the Body of Christ of the benefit. (v. 10)**

3. **You rob God of the glory He deserves. (v. 11)**

One word of caution. Please don't confuse "gifts" with "roles." You have been given roles in your life that are not synonymous with your strengths or gifts, but must be fulfilled. For instance, you may not have a strength in connecting with outsiders and doing evangelism, but that doesn't mean you are excused from doing any evangelism. No doubt, some people are gifted in evangelizing people who aren't Christians, but we are all called to be a witness. We may not be gifted in intercession, but we're all called to pray. We may not have the gift of giving, listed in Romans 12, but we are all called to give offerings and tithes in a local church family. Why? Because all of these activities are Christian roles, not merely gifts.

As you accomplish your mission in life you will want to focus on your strengths, and manage around your weaknesses. You may want to delegate, adding volunteers or staff who are strong where you are weak so that the mission doesn't fail due to your weaknesses. If you have a role (or job) that has several dimensions to it, you don't have to have a strength in each of those dimensions. Excellent performers are seldom well rounded. They fulfill one or two parts of their role well and manage around the others. They fulfill their entire role, but excel at a few portions of it.

I encourage you to locate a "spiritual gifts assessment" at your church or campus ministry, or find suggestions on-line, at: *www.GrowingLeaders.com.* Passion Profile? Other online resources?

The Holy Spirit wants to reveal a supernatural Jesus through your gifts.

Focus on your strengths and manage around your weaknesses.

STEPS TO DISCOVER, DEVELOP AND DISTRIBUTE YOUR STRENGTH

1. EXPLORE…the possibilities.

I recommend you use these years of your life to explore the possibilities open to you. What kind of strengths, what kind of spiritual gifts and what kinds of talents have you observed? Take a spiritual gifts assessment. See if someone at your church or religious group on campus can help you with a spiritual gifts test. Take it and find out what your possibilities are.

2. EXPERIMENT…as much as possible.

Next, start experimenting with your possible gifts by trying out ministry opportunities. Try a bunch of them. When I was in college I got involved in at least a dozen service opportunities—and failed at most of them. But each one enabled me to zero in on my gifts.

3. EXAMINE…your feelings.

Once you've taken these two steps, reflect. How do you feel about what you did? Did you get a sense of deep satisfaction? Did it seem to fit who you are? Or, did it feel uncomfortable? Take some time and journal what you sensed inside your heart of hearts.

4. EVALUATE…your effectiveness.

Next, step back and evaluate any fruit that came from what you did. Were you effective? Did you get results from your ministry activity? If you are in your zone, you will likely see some kind of fruit even though you will need to develop some more.

5. EXPECT…confirmation from the Body.

Finally, listen for confirmation from others. If you serve in your zone the people who know you well and know God well should sense it too. See if they affirm your strengths, and encourage you to keep doing what you tried out as an experiment. May I encourage you to see your church as a "laboratory" where you can begin to experiment now.

Consider this. I am convinced Mother Teresa never tried to be a great leader. She left Albania and made her way to a Catholic girls school to teach in Calcutta. While teaching there she peered outside the windows of the classroom, and she saw the impoverished people on the streets. It broke her heart. She eventually became a principal, but never could

Mother Teresa never tried to be a great leader. She just found her gift and served with it.

Group Up
What are some opportunities you'd like to explore, to see if they match your gifts?

shake her burden for the homeless and destitute in Calcutta. Finally, she went to her priest and begged him to let her go. He refused at first, feeling that her calling was to the school. However, her persistence paid off. She finally convinced everyone on the campus that she was to go and begin a new order, caring for the poor of Calcutta. She went out alone at first and provided a place for the poor and dying to at least receive love and be treated with dignity. Over the years she deepened her influence in the city. Eventually, others joined her effort. By 1979, she had won a Nobel Peace Prize doing things you and I may avoid!

How can this be? She never pursued fame. She never "tried" to be a great leader. She just found her gift and served with it. Along the way, she became one of the most influential women in the world—never seeking that influence. May God do the same for you.

APPLICATION

Write down what you plan to do to use one or more of your spiritual gifts as a student and even after school is done. The plan does not have to be complete and ready for implementation. Talk with God and sketch out the beginning of that plan between you and God to use your gifts.

If you have not yet taken the assessment designed to be part of this "Flourish" package, I invite you to take it. It is called: My Passion Profile. It will enable you to clarify your deepest passions and distinguish them from mere interests. Just go to: www.MyPassionProfile.com.

THE HEART OF A SERVANT

Serving in the Area of Your Gift Will Increase Your Audience

"You know the rulers of the Gentiles lord it over them, and their great men exercise authority over them. It is not so among you, but whoever wishes to be great among you shall be your servant, and whoever wishes to be first among you shall be your slave."
(Matthew 20:25-27)

"All of us are influencing and being influenced simultaneously."

The subject of influence has become vogue over the last decade. Leaders everywhere have become students of influence—how it works, why it works, where to get it and how to leverage it in the lives of clients, employees, customers and members of their congregation. In this chapter we will seek to better understand the concept of influence. We'll spend the majority of our time reviewing the method of influence Jesus models for us as young leaders. Jesus associated leadership with service. He promoted authority or power only when it was motivated by serving others. As far as Jesus is concerned: Leadership without service is a lie. Unfortunately, many students graduate from college—and the first thing on their mind is not service, but climbing a corporate ladder. They'd never admit it, but theirs is a pursuit of power. They say they want to make a difference, but it's all through power.

SEVEN WAYS TO INFLUENCE PEOPLE

Perhaps you've noticed that people influence others everyday. I have said this many times: even introverts will influence approximately 10,000 other people in an average lifetime. We do it intentionally and accidentally, with emotion or with logic, with honey and with vinegar.

The following is a summary of how leaders have influenced people through the ages.

METHODS OF INFLUENCE—FROM WORST TO BEST

FORCE

Influencing others by the use of force is the lowest form of influence. While it is animalistic in nature, humans use force all the time to get others to do

"All of us are influencing and being influenced simultaneously."

what they want. In fact, this is one method utilized not only between individuals, but also between nations. When someone chooses to use force, they push others to do something against their will. People use force when they don't feel they have the time for diplomacy or logic. They want something and are willing to pay the price of severed relationships to get it.

Two Kinds of Force:

Violent – Usually comes in the form of a threat to harm. The recipient feels violated. An illustration of this came in 1990 when Iraq invaded Kuwait, and in 1998 when Serbia began its ethnic cleansing of Kosovo. It is trespassing over the will of another.

Non-violent – Usually comes in the form of coercion. The recipient feels they have no choice in the matter, even though it may only be words that move them. Unhealthy marriages exhibit this when a spouse uses verbal abuse to get his/her way.

Evaluation: How often do you use "force" to influence others? Put a mark on the line below to reflect how often you use "force" to influence others.

Never   1   2   3   4   5   6   Often

INTIMIDATION

In this method the leader is still using unhealthy means to reach his/her end. The motive of the follower is fear of conflict. They simply want to avoid danger or confrontation. Often, leaders use this kind of influence and are unaware of it. It happens every day in the office with supervisors who are short-sighted and low in people skills. The person who intimidates is usually short on both patience and relationships. Frequently, they intimidate because they are insecure and are intimidated themselves. This method shortens and sabotages friendships.

The Good News And The Bad News

The Good News - This method of influence is often the quickest way to get results. Everyone jumps when the leader says to jump.

Intimidation shortens and sabotages friendships.

The Bad News - This method is short lived. It causes turnover in organizations. No healthy person stays in this kind of an environment very long.

Evaluation: How often do you use "intimidation" to influence others? Mark on the line how often you use "intimidation" to influence others.

Never   1   2   3   4   5   6   Often

MANIPULATION

This third method is slightly better, but it's still about a leader taking the low road. With manipulation the follower may technically get to choose his involvement, but still doesn't win. It is a win/lose proposition between the leader and followers. Eventually, the followers feel resentment over the conditions in which they must work. They begin to play the role of a victim and steal time or resources from the organization. They believe they deserve it since they've been treated so poorly. Instead of going the "extra mile" they cheat their way along the first mile.

Characteristics of manipulative leadership
- One person wins; the others lose.
- Control of the situation is one-sided.
- The followers feel they've been taken advantage of by their leader.
- A we/they perspective sets in.
- People begin to be suspicious of each other.
- Partners start vying for power and control.
- There is personal kingdom-building going on.

Evaluation: How often do you use "manipulation" to influence others? Mark on the line how often you use "manipulation" to influence others.

Never   1   2   3   4   5   6   Often

EXCHANGE

This form of influence is neutral. Until now, each kind of influence has been temporarily productive but unhealthy. Using the exchange method, the leader operates with no hidden agenda. There is no need for dam-

Group Up
How have those in authority attempted to influence you?

Group Up

Do you agree with the Chinese proverb that both "horses" (The Mind and The Emotions) must be mobilized in order for the "cart" (The Will) to move forward?

age control. They are simply saying: "I'll scratch your back—and you can scratch my back." That's what exchange is all about; it is give and take. This is probably the most popular form of influence in America today. Millions of Americans show up at work each day not because their boss is motivational or encouraging, but because he/she promised them a paycheck at the end of the month. This kind of influence keeps score and is aware of whose turn it is to give.

The PROS of "exchange": It is fair and just. All parties have agreed to the conditions. It is influence based upon contract. There is no hidden agenda. Everyone gives and receives.

The CONS of "exchange": It only works until one of the parties gets a better exchange somewhere else. It ultimately is still self-serving. All parties look out for their own best interests.

Evaluation: How often do you use "exchange" to influence others? Mark on the line how often you use "exchange" to influence others.

Never   1   2   3   4   5   6   Often

PERSUASION

At this point, our list of "methods of influence" begins to become positive. When a leader persuades a follower to act they frequently use words, like in the methods of manipulation or intimidation. However, with persuasion the follower sees the benefits of working with and for the leader. While it may have taken considerable time for the leader to talk them into it, they are not forced to act; they become hungry to act. They don't have to do it; they want to. Persuasion literally means "through sweetness." The leader has convinced the person with positive words and ideas. The follower is just as convinced as the leader is.

When a person is persuaded they have engaged their entire soul: mind, will, and emotions. It can be understood in the Chinese analogy of the cart and two horses:

> The Will = the Cart
> The Mind = a Horse
> The Emotions = a Horse

If the "cart" is to move forward, both horses must be mobilized. So it is with the heart of man. This is why Proverbs tells us to *"trust in the Lord with all of your heart…"*

Evaluation: How often do you use "persuasion" to influence others? Mark on the line how often you use "persuasion" to influence others.

Never   1   2   3   4   5   6   **Often**

MOTIVATION

From a purely human standpoint this is the highest type of influence. It has been said that people are naturally motivated, but as we age we become de-motivated. We need someone to help us tap into our inner yearning to do something significant. The leader who motivates others understands that the people really do want to act, but simply need some other human (outside) motivation to get up and do it. Action becomes the result of inward desire plus outward stimulation. This explains the huge market for motivational speakers and resources in the business world. The information presented isn't necessarily new, but it engages their passion and longing to do something great. When a husband says, "I love you" to his wife, it is motivating to her. Why? It is not new information. However, the message engages her soul with words she needs and wants to hear.

Describe a personal example and share the outcome.

The word *motivate* is taken from the same root as *movement.* We are moved when a leader speaks to our inward…

- **NEEDS** (Things we need in our day-to-day life)

- **INTERESTS** (Things we're curious about or have an interest in)

- **CONCERNS** (Things we are concerned about or fearful of)

- **DESIRES** (Things we deeply want in our heart of hearts)

Being broken transforms the leader from a "boss" to a humble servant.

Evaluation: How often do you use "motivation" to influence others? Mark on the line how often you use "motivation" to influence others.

Never   1   2   3   4   5   6   **Often**

SPIRITUAL AUTHORITY

This is the highest form of influence in the Body of Christ. Not everyone has it, nor is it easy to wrap your arms around. It is influence derived from the life of the leader as well as from the presence of God. When a leader has spiritual authority God prompts His people to act through that leader, but it is divine. It is not dependent upon eloquence—just ask Moses. It is not dependent upon being tall and rugged—just ask David. It is not dependent upon having a brilliant or trained mind—just ask Simon Peter. When a leader has authority, people act knowing that they are linking up with something and Someone bigger than themselves or the leader. The influence, in fact, can be frightening to the leader. They know it's bigger than they are and it can be abused. This is why God so often chooses to break a leader before He uses him profoundly. Our Lord knows power can be entrusted only to those who are conformed to His image. Being broken transforms the leader from a "boss" to a humble servant. Consequently, we most often see spiritual authority flowing from a leader who is committed to serving those who follow. In fact, I believe we can have spiritual authority even with unbelievers. They won't call it by that name, but when we serve others in the marketplace, and do it with competence, we gain authority in their lives.

SPIRITUAL AUTHORITY STEMS FROM:

Honoring and serving people - David got his authority this way with his mighty men. They began as distressed and discontented men, but ended up being called "mighty men of valor" (1 Chronicles 12). How were they so transformed? David modeled servant leadership for them. He honored them.

Question: How do you model servanthood to others? Do you honor those you lead?

Anointing and God's Presence - Joseph got his authority this way. All along the way—from the pit to the prison to the palace, the Scriptures kept saying: "But God was with Joseph…" (Genesis 39:2). People could sense the presence of God and the anointing on his life to do something great. It was evident.

Question: Is God's anointing evident in your life? Do people sense God's presence?

Group Up
Daniel's gift made him competent for each challenge. How are you serving with your gift?

Giftedness and Competency - Daniel got his authority this way. Whenever kings did not know what to do they called their magicians. And when the magicians couldn't figure it out, they called on Daniel (Daniel 2). His gift made him competent for each challenge facing the nation. Daniel chose to serve with that gift.

Question: Do you have an evident leadership gift? Do people look to you for direction?

Conviction and Passion - Paul got at least part of his authority this way. While he was a man with a brilliant mind and a servant's heart, people followed his passion. He had spiritual convictions that won the respect of those who even disagreed with him including Pharisees and Centurions.

Question: Do your convictions win the respect of others? Do people follow your passion?

Evaluation: How often do use "spiritual authority" to influence others? Mark on the line how often you use "spiritual authority" to influence others.

Never   1   2   3   4   5   6   **Often**

INFLUENCE IN THE BIBLE

Influence shows up vividly in the Scriptures:

We are commanded to manage our influence with others (Colossians 4:5-6).

We are called "salt" and "light" in the world, implying influence on it (Matthew 5:13-14).

We are told not to be influenced by evil, but to influence the evil (Romans 12:21).

The apostle Paul was forthright and unashamed regarding his ambition to influence others for the kingdom of God: "Knowing, then, the fear of the Lord, we persuade people…" (2 Corinthians 5:11).

I underscore this because today we often shrink from trying to influence others. We are sensitive to the negative face of power; to the pressure to

Group Up
Which of these seven forms of influence have you used most often? Why?

be politically correct and to tolerate others rather than to change them. We fear it will be perceived as manipulation. It seems we need a reminder of the conscious pursuit of influence among the early church leaders.

My point is simply this. The leaders of the New Testament were determined to influence people, but they did so by honoring them. The most influential people in the New Testament were those who served others. Paul was driven to influence people for Christ, but he did so first by serving them. In the book of Acts the same is true for Barnabas. Peter taught this to his leaders in 1 Peter 5:1-4. So did John in his three letters. And, of course, Jesus modeled this kind of servant leadership when He washed the feet of His disciples. Serving the twelve was His final ministry before He went to His trial and crucifixion. Each one seemed to know this truth: we lead by serving and we serve by leading. If you are serious about living a life of influence, you must choose a lifestyle of service.

It is said that every Wednesday morning Toshiko Yamamoto takes a washbasin and towel to the roughest part of Vancouver, British Columbia. There she washes the feet of women at a drop-in center. Her clients are often infected with HIV or Hepatitis C. Their feet are dirty and covered with sores and needle marks. The women are almost always drug addicts who sell sex to pay for their next fix. As Toshiko gently washes and massages their feet she sings a lullaby in Japanese, listens to their stories, and tells them about God's love. "Men treat them as garbage," she observes. "I do the opposite."

Toshiko is among a growing number of Christians who've decided the best way to influence the horrible downtown area of Vancouver is by serving. One group offers free hairstyling and manicures. Another welcomes these women into a safe house for drug rehabilitation. Other groups are focusing on the men who also deal with addictive behavior. Some offer job training, meals and places to come for coffee and a listening ear. All of this has begun to transform the area. The complexion of downtown Vancouver is being impacted by these ordinary people. They're leaders. You can explain their influence however you want, but I call it spiritual authority. It's achieved through serving—people serving people in the area of their gifts. That's the best way to do it. A good title for this type of influence is the art of strategic service.

If you are serious about living a life of influence, you must choose a lifestyle of service.

REFLECT AND RESPOND
Who do you have authority with in your life?

Make a short list of how you got it.
1.
2.
3.
4.

A CASE STUDY ON STRATEGIC SERVICE: ANDREW

Let's take a look at a good example of this issue from the New Testament. His name is Andrew, an unsung hero who happened to be one of Jesus' disciples. The Bible doesn't tell us a lot about Andrew. You can count on your fingers the number of times he is mentioned specifically. But what the Bible does tell us about him shows that he had the right heart for strategic service. His authority and influence came through serving others.

A friend, Phil Johnson, got me thinking about these thoughts years ago, and I share them with you here to give you perspective. Andrew's ministry was characterized by four significant insights that the other disciples had trouble grasping.

1. The Value of Individual People

Andrew knew the value of individual people. While several of the disciples were focused on the crowds and even preached to large crowds in their ministries, Andrew was into people— one life at a time. He brought individuals not crowds to the Lord. Almost every time we see him, Andrew is serving someone individually. Check out John 1:41-42 and John 12:20-22.

Both Andrew and his brother Peter had hearts for ministry, but their methods were very different. Peter preached at Pentecost, which was a landmark sermon in church history. Yet it was Andrew who had individually introduced Peter to Jesus.

Dwight Moody, the great evangelist of the 19th century spoke to thousands all over the world. Yet it's said that it was Mr. Kimball, an unknown

---

Serving the 12 disciples was Jesus' final ministry before He faced the cross.

One by one, Andrew brought individuals, not crowds, to the Lord.

97 - FLOURISH

shoe salesman, who introduced Dwight Moody to Christ. Mr. Kimball witnessed to him one-on-one. He knew the value of individual people. Do you remember the classic little story of the starfish? An old man was walking along the beach one morning, picking up starfish, gazing at their beauty, then throwing them back into the water. When a jogger happened by he asked the man what he was doing. The old man said he was enjoying the beauty of each starfish, one by one. Then he was throwing them back into the water so they would live. Instantly, the jogger laughed and said, "I can't believe you'd take the time to do that. There are thousands of these starfish on this beach. You'll never get to them all. What difference does it make?" In that moment the old man threw a starfish into the water. When he did he simply pointed at it and replied, "It made a difference to that one."

> **Question:** How do you demonstrate the value of individual people through your life? Think about it. If you have an accountability partner, share your thoughts with that person. You can always share your thoughts with Christ.

2. The Value of Inconspicuous Service
Andrew could have had more visibility. He was among the first disciples chosen, and he was a leader of sorts. But he was content to labor in the shadows.

Consider this: Andrew was Peter's brother, and he knew him as well as anyone. He surely knew that if he brought Peter into the group of disciples Peter would become the leader. He would probably take over with his personality. That didn't matter to Andrew. It wasn't his style to seek personal glory. His goal was "good" not "glory."

During my college years I'll never forget preparing to go into the ministry. I had visions of speaking to huge crowds, just like Billy Graham. My roommate, John, was a talented vocalist, and we thought we'd make a great team: singer and speaker. One weekend he was asked to come to Dallas to sing at a church and he invited me to come along. All the way down to Dallas I thought I'd better get ready to speak, because when this church realized we were a team and I planned to become a pastor, they would want me minister as well. When we arrived John did his microphone check and warm up. I patiently waited for the senior pastor to acknowledge my existence and invite me to do something. I waited and waited and waited. Finally, I decided to take matters into my own hands. I approached the pastor, shook his hand and introduced myself as John's roommate. In fact, I told him we were a team. (Surely he would get the hint!) Then, I politely asked him what he'd like me to do. I was hardly prepared for his answer. He thought for a minute, and then he said, "I'll tell you what. John is probably going to get a little warm as he sings. While he sings, why don't you hold his coat."

I was dumbfounded. With all my talent, this man was asking me to hold my roommate's coat! As I look back on that day I see how God used it to break me. My talent wasn't as big as I thought and it certainly wasn't the issue at that point in my life. God didn't want my talent until He controlled my heart. I discovered the litmus test of whether or not you are a servant is how you act when you are treated like one. Everyone wants to be thought of as a servant—no one wants to be treated like one.

That day led to a whole new perspective. I began to watch God open up marvelous doors as I stopped lobbying for fame and started laboring in the shadows, with no spotlight or microphones. Some months later I was on the streets with a friend, sharing Christ with some guys who were sitting on the hoods of their cars, drinking. We approached one group and introduced ourselves. We told them we were out just talking to people about their faith and asking if they had a relationship with God. One of them spoke up and began cussing at us. He told us to get out of his blankety-blank life and that he didn't want to talk about our blankety-blank religion. It was obvious that this was our cue to move on.

As we started to walk away the guy who'd just cussed us out began complaining about his back. He said he had hurt it on the job, and that his blankety-blank boss made him work with a bad back. As he spoke to his friends I sensed God speaking to me. The Lord was leading me back to this group to pray for this guy. Needless to say, that was the last thing I wanted to do, especially after he'd just told us to get out of his life!

I turned around out of sheer obedience and reluctantly interrupted this guy. I asked him if I could pray for his back. There was dead silence. He didn't know how to respond. So before he could, I just explained that no matter what they believed I believed in the power of prayer and that the

The litmus test of whether or not you are a servant is how you act when you are treated like one.

Bible tells us to lay hands on the sick and pray for them. So I did. It was hilarious—all the guys scampered to put down their beer cans and take off their baseball hats. When I finished praying for this guy he stood up immediately and yelled out: "What did you do to me?"

A little nervous, I responded, "Nothing! I promise. I didn't do anything to you!" Fortunately, God had done something. This guy began to swear that his pain was gone…that he could stand up straight! He was astounded. It was the only time I'd ever heard a testimony of the power of God with cuss words in it! Everyone was amazed—and needless to say, we now had everyone's attention in that little gang of guys covered in leather and chains. I discovered that little prayer—that little act of service—started a sequence of events that led to several of those guys coming to Christ.

Question: What private acts of service do you provide to others?

3. The Value of Insignificant Gifts

Andrew also understood the value of little gifts. When the disciples were fretting about how to feed five thousand people one day, it was Andrew who brought the boy with the loaves and fish to Jesus (John 6:8-9). He knew no gift was insignificant once it reached the hands of Jesus. God can certainly create miracles out of nothing, but He often chooses to use "starters" or little insignificant gifts we bring to begin the process. It was a staff in Moses' hand that started a miracle; it was a jar of oil in Elijah's hand that started a miracle.

Andrew didn't stop to rationalize, or he might have never acted. When we argue that we don't have much to give—it won't make any difference—we never get the miracle started. Andrew heard Jesus talk about the value of insignificant gifts when He taught the lesson about the widow's mite in Mark 12:41-44. The lesson sank in and Andrew spent his life watching his seemingly small gifts expand in God's hands.

I once heard a story about a lady named Stella. Stella was 80 years old and she was blind. She was also confined to her little condominium. One day she groaned to God that she wished He would just take her home. God responded to her prayer by impressing on her that as long as she was alive, He wasn't finished with her yet. In her mind this was a ridiculous thought. She reminded God that she was 80, blind as a bat and stuck in her home. He reminded her that she still had a voice, a telephone and a gift of connecting with people. Stella had always been good at relationships. She sat in silence for quite some time, thinking. With that reminder Stella decided she would do what she could, even though it wasn't much.

The next morning, she woke up and opened her Braille telephone book. Beginning with the As, then the Bs, then the Cs, she began to call individuals and get acquainted. She began by saying, "Hello. My name is Stella. I am 80 years old and I'm blind—that's why I'm not at your door right now. I just wanted you to know that I started a relationship with God many years ago that has changed my life. I wondered if I could share this with you? Do you have a relationship with God?"

When I first heard Stella's story I was in a group of people who were asking her how folks responded to her phone calls. Stella just smiled and told us she heard words she'd never heard before! We all laughed. But when someone suggested that it must have been difficult to get rejected like that. Stella stopped them. "Oh no," she argued. "That was nothing compared to the fact that I've been able to introduce 8,000 people to Christ in the last nine years."

Question: What gifts do you have to offer others?

REFLECT AND RESPOND

When we put these three values together, we have a powerful combination. Think about a time when you combined the value of individual people, the value of inconspicuous service and the value of insignificant gifts you have to offer. How did you do it? Remember how God used my prayer for the man with the bad back? What's your story like? Briefly jot it down in the space allotted below.

Where do you believe your most strategic service takes place? Is it on campus? At work? With your family? With friends?

Group Up
When was the last time you offered an act of service to someone anonymously?

The reason serving others is so powerful is because it is love triumphing over power.

LOVE VS. POWER

Consider one more thought. If you are not convinced that strategic service is the best way to invest your life, perhaps this truth will persuade you.

Another way to communicate what I've tried to say in this chapter is to see it as love vs. power. Most people choose to pursue power if they want to influence the world. It is the way of the world. It seems like the only way to really get something done. Meekness is too much like weakness, and we argue that no one really seems to respond to weakness. Instead, many believe if we Christians can just gain power in the world of business, politics and entertainment, we can make those arenas change. The key is power!

I don't think Jesus would agree. If power is the key—He certainly obtained it in a far different way than His people do today. Jesus never pursued power. He always pursued love. In fact, I contend that we cannot pursue power and love at the same time. Jesus will come as a lion one day, but He came first as a lamb. As He pursued love He laid down His rights and power willingly. Interestingly, love eventually wins…and gains power for the one who loves. But we cannot pursue it. Power is a by-product of love.

Think about the civil rights movement in the 1960s. Dr. Martin Luther King knew that it could not succeed if the movement chose to pursue power, as the Black Panthers did. He chose love and non-violence…which eventually won people over. But it was the pursuit of love not power that won. Pursuing power is an immediate, short-term way to bring about change. It is short-lived. Love ultimately wins in the long run because it builds trust and adds value to people.

The reason serving others is so powerful is because it is love triumphing over power. It is the Church choosing not to push and shove for control, but surrendering that control in the name of love. Maybe this is what Jesus meant when He said, "The gentle… will inherit the earth" (Matthew 5:5). Maybe this is what He meant by saying things like, "If you want to save your life, you must lose it; if you want to the greatest, you must be a servant; if you want to be strong, you must be weak; if you want to live you must die" (See Matthew 16:25, 20:26; Luke 9:24).

WHAT ARE WE TO DO?

A number of years ago Norman Cousins reported a conversation he had on a trip to India. He was talking with a Hindu priest named Satis Prasad. The man said he wanted to come to our country to work as a missionary among Americans. Cousins assumed that he meant that he wanted to convert Americans to the Hindu religion, but when asked Satis Prasad said, "Oh no. I would like to convert them to the Christian religion. Christianity cannot survive in the abstract. It needs not membership but believers. The people of your country may claim they believe in Christianity, but from what I read at this distance, Christianity is more of a custom than anything else. I would ask that either you accept the teachings of Jesus in your everyday life and in your affairs as a nation, or stop invoking His name as a sanction for everything you want to do. I want to save Christianity for the Christian."

That's a good word for us today. We either buy in to the Person and the ways of Jesus, or we don't. If we do, we'd best get a water basin and a towel and prove it.

ASSESSMENT

Evaluate your heart. Do you have a servant's heart? Check all that apply.

○ Yes   ○ Most of the time   ○ Sometime   ○ Not usually   ○ No

Jot down at least two ways of demonstrating how you show a servant's heart in your life.

1.

2.

When do you believe you are most strategic in your service?

"I want to save Christianity for the Christian."

We either buy into the Person and the ways of Jesus or we don't.

How do your gifts fit into helping you have a servant's heart? Jot some thoughts down below.

APPLICATION

Name one action step you can take this week on your campus to implement strategic service. If not on campus, how about in your home? With friends? At work?

BUILDING HEALTHY EMOTIONS

Becoming Secure Will Increase Stamina and Stability

"Guard your heart above all else, for it is the source of life."
(Proverbs 4:23)

PERSONAL INSECURITY PREVENTS EFFECTIVE LEADERSHIP

During the term of President Ronald Reagan, leaders from seven industrial nations were meeting at the White House to discuss economic policy. Reagan has recounted that during the meeting he came across Canadian Prime Minister Pierre Trudeau who was strongly upbraiding British Prime Minister Margaret Thatcher. He was criticizing her, telling her that she was wrong and that her policies wouldn't work. She stood there in front of him with her head up, listening until he was finished. Then she walked away.

Following the confrontation Reagan approached her and said, "Maggie, he should never have spoken to you like that. He was entirely out of line. Why did you let him get away with that?"

Thatcher answered, "A woman must know when a man is simply being childish."

That story surely typifies Margaret Thatcher. It takes a strong, secure person to succeed as a world leader. And that is especially true when the person is a woman. As a world leader, Thatcher experienced much criticism. At one point she was referred to as "the most unpopular woman in Britain." But she didn't waver under the criticism. She remained secure in her convictions and maintained her self-respect. She once said, "To me, consensus seems to be the process of abandoning all beliefs, principles, values, and policies in search of something in which no one believes . . . What great cause would have been fought and won under the banner, 'I stand for consensus'?" Because of her security in both herself and her leadership, the "Iron Lady," as she was called, was elected to three consecutive terms as prime minister. She is the only British leader of the modern era ever to achieve that status.

"What great cause would have been fought and won under the banner, 'I stand for consensus'?"

THE FACT OF THE MATTER

A leader's sense of emotional security will either stabilize or sabotage him/her more than anything else. Unfortunately, colleges and graduate schools cannot teach us to possess personal security and identity. Many of them fail to even address the topic, assuming those issues are already resolved in the hearts of the men and women who enter the program. But they are not. Leaders in all fields struggle with personal insecurity. Note the following statistics gathered from surveys of Christian pastors.

70% of pastors said their self-image is lower now than when they entered the ministry.

95% of pastors say they don't have the leadership gifts to perform in the way their congregations expect them to perform.

75% of pastors responded anonymously that they are intimidated by the lay leaders or staff with which they work.

65% of pastors said they seriously considered quitting the ministry in the last two months.

REFLECT AND RESPOND

Why must leaders develop a strong sense of security? Have you ever served under an insecure leader? What was it like?

TO PUT IT GRAPHICALLY

Study the diagram below. Each one of us has inner needs that require attention. If we assume a position of leadership without addressing these needs in healthy ways, we may experience a "train wreck" within our own personal lives...often in public. Personal security is essential to effective leadership.

Inner need:	If missing, we feel:	Common symptoms:
Belonging	Insecure	Over-compensation, emotional highs and lows
Worth	Inferior	Competition, self-doubt, need for recognition
Competence	Inadequate	Comparison with specific people; defensive attitude
Purpose	Insignificant	Compulsive, driven spirit, defeat, depression

REFLECT AND RESPOND
Examine the inner needs and the common symptoms if they go unmet. At work, in school, or at home, which of these behaviors exhibit themselves in different pockets of your life? Reflect on the chart above and put a check by the symptoms you display. Now describe how you act out these symptoms in your behavior. (I cut others down; I try to "one up" my friends; I focus unduly upon myself in relationship and conversation, and so forth.) Space below is given for you to share.

Group Up
Discuss which inner need you struggle with the most.

SPOTTING INSECURITY IN YOUR BEHAVIOR
We all have personal insecurities. When we approach new situations it is normal to ask yourself, "Do I have what it takes to meet this new challenge?" But there is a kind of day-to-day insecurity in the life of many leaders. It prohibits them from seeing themselves correctly and therefore from seeing others around them correctly. This insecurity often dilutes the leader's results. It happens every day. To be honest, personal insecurity is fairly easy to spot in our behavior. We fail to see it merely because we ignore it. We pretend it isn't there by defending ourselves and diverting the focus on to something else. The following are six biblical case studies of ordinary people who struggled with different, common insecurities. Notice how it showed up in their lives. Then, reflect on your own life and see if you identify with those symptoms.

SIX SYMPTOMS OF INSECURITY

1. Comparison
We compare ourselves to others and score ourselves against their achievements.

The Parable of the Vineyard Workers
An example of this symptom occurs in Matthew 20 where Jesus tells the story of the vineyard workers. Take a minute to read this parable from Matthew 20 in your Bible. Then reflect on areas where you have exhibited attitudes of comparison to others.

Three Insecure Actions

1. I can't celebrate with those who succeed.

2. I get defensive about my own accomplishments.

3. I project my self-worth onto others.

Take a moment to honestly evaluate how you would act out personal security or insecurity if you were one of the vineyard workers that day. Those workers teach us five truths. When you compare...

1. You ignore God's grace to you, being preoccupied with the status of others.
2. You grumble and complain about perceived inequities.
3. You judge others as less worthy of blessing than you.
4. You assume you deserve more because your focus is in your work, not God's.
5. You forget that all reward and blessing is due to the grace of God.

REFLECT AND RESPOND

Examine the three insecure actions listed on the sidebar. Take a minute and briefly write about a situation in your life that caused you to experience one of these reactions. How did you feel...how did you respond... what made you respond this way?

2. Compensation

We feel like victims and must now compensate for our losses or inferiority.

Compensation is very familiar to us in today's society. People often fall into the grips of materialism in an effort to compensate for a weakness in their life. Sometimes men use expensive cars or lavish houses to make up for a perceived inferiority. Women can become obsessive about their appearance to compensate for some other deficiency—even to the point of developing an eating disorder. Leaders will do odd things to compensate for or cover up their deficiencies.

Jacob's life - Insecurity is not a new idea; it has been around since the beginning of time. The Old Testament patriarch Jacob experienced it. Inspect Jacob's life and see what you can learn about your own insecurities as you read Genesis 27 and 32. See if you can discover some of Jacob's insecurities, especially as they pertain to compensation. What words would you use to describe his behavior? You can jot them down here for easy reference.

REFLECT AND RESPOND

If, at the end of Jacob's life we were able to listen to his thoughts as he reflected upon this early stage of his life, we might hear him making these five observations about compensation. See if any of them might be true of you at your present stage of life.

1. We scheme how to get ahead and how to gain recognition.
2. We begin to depend on personal politics to advance ourselves.
3. We fail to recognize God's blessing on us because of our pursuit for more.
4. We fight irrational battles to get what we think we deserve.
5. We may stoop to dishonesty and deception to get results.

When have you demonstrated any of these actions in your life and leadership? Take a moment and write out a brief prayer asking God to forgive you for specific times when these actions characterized how you felt or how you acted.

3. Competition

We become self-centered, determined to outdo others to gain attention or rewards.

A third symptom of insecurity is competition. When we honestly examine the motivation for the decisions that we make in leadership, too often we find that these decisions were motivated by competition. The competition might come from someone who is positioned under us and who we believe we must suppress. Or it might come from a friend or a peer who we believe we must surpass.

Group Up

Share some situations that demonstrate healthy vs. harmful competition.

Healthy vs. Harmful Competition

Now, just to clarify, there is both healthy competition and harmful competition. Healthy competition challenges both you and your competitor, sharpens both your skills, and results in a win-win situation. Michael Jordan would never have achieved his greatness without an extremely competitive spirit. I was reading a *Sports Illustrated* article detailing Michael's personal life, and it relayed how he competes in everything that he does. There is nothing he enjoys more in his free time than competing at ping-pong, pool, or another sport in his vast recreation room. He is extremely competitive, but his competitive fire is not fueled by insecurity. Harmful competition, by contrast, is rooted in insecurity. It is driven by the feelings that we must be first and others must be below us. It strives for a win-lose outcome where I must be at the center, or be the best, or get rewarded the most. When it comes to having a harmful competitive spirit, the older brother of the prodigal son would have given anyone a run for their money (Luke 15:11-31).

The "Older" Prodigal Son

Read Luke 15, the story of the prodigal son. In verses 28-30 try to spot some of the older brother's competitive words or actions. What are some similarities you see in both sons?

REFLECT AND RESPOND

Drop in on an imaginary conversation between the older son and his counselor. After hearing the personal struggles with insecurity he experienced, his therapist might have pointed out these negative competitive tendencies he was demonstrating. See if they sound familiar to you.

You tend to keep score on life.
You tend to be ungrateful.
You tend to be unteachable.
You tend to get jealous for recognition.
You tend to be prideful.
You tend to be critical and judgmental.
You tend to be loveless.
You tend to live a self-centered life.

4. Compulsion
You are driven to perform compulsively to gain others' approval; you're a people-pleaser.

Ironically, in a society where we cherish our personal freedom to make decisions, the fourth symptom of insecurity strips away much of that freedom. It is easy to fall into the people-pleaser trap and to try to find our identity in what others think of us rather than in what God thinks of us. There is no better example of this than Martha's story in the New Testament.

Martha's Life
Read Luke 10:38-42, the story of Martha's dinner party for Jesus. Notice how her activity was motivated by her compulsive spirit, not by love for her Savior. Why do you think that Jesus was not impressed by her "performance?"

REFLECT AND RESPOND
Let's look again at the imaginary conversation Martha had with her counselor about her compulsive tendencies. The counselor would have helped her realize that...

> *She was distracted from "big picture" priorities, consumed by her own performance.*
> *She projected her self-worth to others and over-estimated her importance.*
> *She experienced self-pity and sought recognition for her hard work.*
> *She grew weary because she attempted to do too much—for the wrong reasons.*
> *She tended to be a perfectionist.*

You might recognize some of these characteristics if you have a propensity for slipping into a compulsive mindset. If you have found yourself in this mindset, ask God to help you overcome this insecurity. What people, situations, past experiences, or feelings cause you to fall into this performance trap?

Group Up
Describe how you have fallen into the "performance trap."

5. Condemnation
The judgmental attitude of yourself/others, resulting in self-pity or self-conceit.

Another type of symptom we may experience is condemnation. This type of insecurity manifests itself most often in our attitude. The prophet Elijah demonstrated this attitude during a difficult season in his ministry. Read 1 Kings 19, the story of Elijah fleeing after his encounter with the prophets of Baal. Join Elijah as he hosts a pity party, with himself as the star attraction. Then, interact to see if you've ever thrown a pity party like his.

As you read, think about how you suppose Elijah could plunge from a total victory in 1 Kings 18 to total despair in 1 Kings 19? How could this happen? If you have an accountability partner, this would be excellent to share with each other.

REFLECT AND RESPOND
While finishing up the counseling session with Martha, imagine Elijah walking into the room and honestly sharing his attitude. He might confess something like this…

> *I have a shortsighted perception of my circumstances.*
> *I feel self-pity and loneliness, as though I'm the only one to endure hardship.*
> *I complain about unjust circumstances and feel overwhelmed.*
> *I fear my demise and insignificance.*
> *I either project neurosis or a character disorder, blaming myself or others for everything that is wrong.*

If you recognize some of these attitudes and actions, meditate on Philippians 4:8 - "Summing it all up, friends, I'd say you'll do best by filling your minds and meditating on things true, noble, reputable, authentic, compelling, gracious—the best, not the worst; the beautiful, not ugly; things to praise, not things to curse" (*The Message*).

God's perspective on this symptom is found in 1 Corinthians 4:3-5: "It matters very little to me what you think of me, even less where I rank in popular opinion. I don't even rank myself. Comparison in these matters are pointless...The Master makes that judgment. So don't get ahead of the Master and jump to conclusions with your judgments before all the evidence is in. When He comes, He will bring out in the open and place in evidence all kinds of things we never even dreamed of—inner motives and purposes and prayers. Only then will any one of us get to hear the 'Well done!' of God"*(The Message)*.

6. Control
In order to validate your own worth, you feel as though you must take charge, protect your own interests and monopolize situations.

The sixth symptom of insecurity that can cripple our leadership is the need for control. Our need for control is often evidenced by our trying to run another person's agenda or by our manipulating relationships to get what we want from them. In the Old Testament, Sarah's life evidenced the need for control. When she became uncertain of God's promise she took control of the situation and tried to bring about God's will by her own means. Read Genesis 16:1-6 and see if your behavior ever resembles Sarah's. Examine thoughts, words, or actions you identify with in this account as she attempted to control her situation.

Do you relate most to Jacob, Martha, Elijah, or Sarah? Why?

REFLECT AND RESPOND
Had Sarah stepped back from her dilemma and evaluated her feelings and actions, she might have seen her controlling behavior. If she did, she would have seen that...

> *She felt God was inattentive, absent or even against her.*
> *Her circumstances determined her understanding of God's character.*
> *She viewed life as scarce rather than abundant.*
> *She became self-seeking and manipulative of others.*
> *She felt intimidated and she dealt with others through intimidation.*
> *She resented the success of others and even turned on them in anger.*
> *She felt if someone succeeds, then someone else must lose.*
> *She frequently blamed others for her dilemma.*

We just examined the six symptoms of insecurity and are ready to take great strides in our development of personal security. To refresh your memory, look back at the six symptoms and remember which ones you most identified with. Now, let's look at what to do when insecurity raises its ugly head.

As leaders, our struggle with personal security often comes and goes. We feel as if we've won the war during times of success or popularity among the people we lead. However, insecurity raises its ugly head when things aren't going well. Below are several circumstances that tend to reveal insecurity. Do any trigger insecurity in you?

Criticism and rejection
> When colleagues or subordinates attack our performance or character.

Meeting someone important
> When we're first introduced to someone we feel we must impress.

Failure at an assignment
> When we fail to reach a goal or standard, we take it personally.

A colleague's success
> When a peer achieves notoriety and reward for their own success.

Unrecognized achievement
> When people we respect fail to notice our success and accomplishment.

Personal loss
> When people and resources we've relied upon are taken away.

Reflecting on an unfair past
> When we become melancholy about our own victimized, unjust background.

Unfamiliar territory
> When we find ourselves in a new and unfamiliar situation.

REFLECT AND RESPOND
When have these scenarios sparked feelings of insecurity in you? Describe the situation.

REAL LIFE
When I first became a pastor, at age 19, I met a colleague who struggled with insecurity. He told me that the board of elders at his church intimidated him. Then, he told me the church congregation intimidated him. I

Group Up
Identify the symptoms that best describe your insecurities.

listened for an hour to the stories he told about his low self-esteem. He constantly lived with intimidation and anxiety. He was always second-guessing himself.

That conversation shed light on the events at his church over the next four years. The church almost split. Board meetings were cruel and angry. In fact, the church would have split had they not fired my friend from his position.

What's sad about this story is this. It wasn't that he was a bad pastor or had poor people skills or theology. It was simply a story of a leader with emotional deficits who sabotaged his leadership.

THE LIES WE BELIEVE

It is possible to waffle between the six symptoms and even experience several at the same time. The key to successfully handling insecurity is to identify how we cope with our insecurity, and what kind of lies we tell ourselves about the reality we face.

Consider this: If the truth makes us free (John 8:32), then lies put us in bondage. The level of defeat and bondage we face as leaders may be directly linked to the volume of myths or lies we've embraced about our identity. Our problem is that while we know the truth...we often believe the lie. Dr. Chris Thurman has written an insightful book entitled, The Lies We Believe. He provides a helpful process for us to understand.

HOW TO STEP INTO THE TRUTH

Determine the trigger event that fostered the lie/bondage.

Example: Your supervisor failed to affirm the hard work you put in on last week's successful event. You feel resentful and insignificant.

These steps are integral to freeing you from wrong thinking. What is an event that triggered insecurity within you? Write it below:

Discover the lie you've believed about that situation.

Example: Perhaps you've embraced the lie, "I am only as good as what I do." You've attached your value to performance and the approval of others.

What current lie have you believed in this situation?

Decide what response is truthful, appropriate and realistic.
What is your truthful, appropriate, and realistic response to this event and lie?

Example: My personal worth is tied to who I am not what I do. My supervisor does appreciate me, but is human like me and likely failed to notice my work due to an oversight. After all, he has been very busy himself.

"You will know the truth, and the truth will free you" (John 8:32).

KEYS TO PERSONAL SECURITY
In the final pages of this lesson, we will examine four keys to personal security:
1. Identity
2. Brokenness
3. Purpose
4. Giving and Receiving "The Blessing"

Study each key and embrace the truth completely. This may be the beginning of a wonderful leadership journey...where we each can be prevented from sabotaging ourselves and our leadership due to personal insecurities.

Key One: IDENTITY
You must tie your self-worth to your identity in Christ, not people or performance.
Our security lies in our identifying who God wired us to be. This means recognizing our unique strengths and gifts, as well as the resources He placed in us, now that we are "in Christ." Every believer—and certainly every leader—must settle this issue.

Key Two: BROKENNESS
You must allow God to break you of self-sufficiency and self-promotion.
The second key to developing security is brokenness. We all want the grace and blessing of God on our lives. But, God "gives grace to the humble." Brokenness is the pathway to experience what we really want and need. If I am not broken by God, I will continue to resolve my insecurities with my own strength and old patterns. Jacob wrestled with God for twenty years before finally learning the essentials of His grace and blessing.

Key Three: PURPOSE
You must identify your God-given purpose in life, and not imitate someone else.
The third key to our security is purpose. Just as Jesus was sent with a specific mission to accomplish, so we are sent to accomplish a specific purpose with each of our lives. We are to link our lives with God's purposes for the world.

Key Four: GIVING and RECEIVING "THE BLESSING"
We must learn to let others love and bless us and do the same for them.
The fourth and final key to developing personal security is giving and receiving "the blessing." In the Old and New Testaments fathers would "bless" their sons. This was more than just a simple prayer for them. It was a display of affection, it was a passing of authority and an expression of faith in that son. In one sense, it was a rite of passage into manhood. The Blessing consisted of five ingredients:

> *Spoken word* — We need to be affirmed by others.
> *Meaningful touch* — We need to be embraced and touched by others.
> *Expression of high value* — We need to have our strengths recognized.
> *Vision of a special future* — We need someone to believe in our future.
> *Application of genuine commitment* — We need someone to follow through on this blessing.

If the truth sets us free, then lies put us in bondage.

THE ROOT OF THE PROBLEM

These four keys address the needs we all have inside. I have watched myself become secure as a leader when I settled them in my own life. Our root issue is diagramed below. Our behavior and habits are only a demonstration of what is happening below the surface in our hearts. When we get beyond the surface we see that at the root of our struggle is the issue of self-worth. Items above it are symptomatic of this deeper issue. In our behavior we first spot negative patterns. Just below the surface we can identify negative attitudes or emotions. If we dig deeper we most often see the issue of unforgiveness. Even deeper is the issue of unmet needs. When someone fails to meet our needs we cannot forgive them. Ultimately, the very root of the problem, the real issue is self-worth.

Four Keys to Personal Security:

1. *Identity*
2. *Brokenness*
3. *Purpose*
4. *Giving and Receiving "The Blessing"*

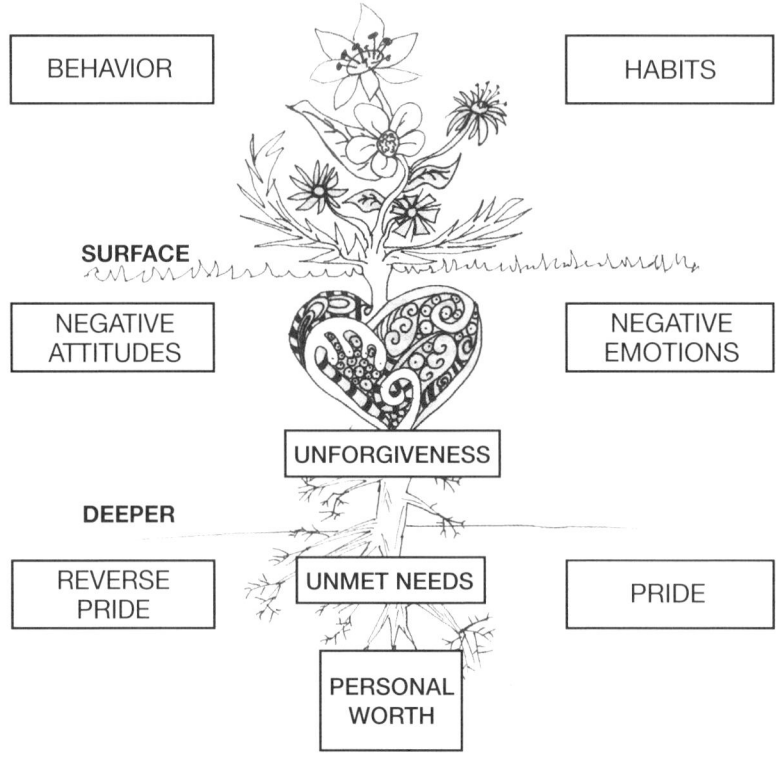

TRUTHS TO LIVE BY:

Never put your emotional health in the hands of someone else.

The truth is a requirement for spiritual and emotional health.

Most of our unhappiness and insecurity is the result of lies we believe.

Recognize that you will believe what you want to believe.

The truth can be eclipsed by a thrilling lie.

A secret to healthy living is negotiating and balancing life's hardships.

Remember that hurting people naturally hurt people; intimidated people intimidate. We can only pass on what we possess.

ASSESS YOURSELF

Reflect back on the lesson as a whole and evaluate how secure you are as a person and as a leader. When a follower has a great idea, do you suppress it or support it? Do you celebrate your people's victories, or do you try to "one-up" them because you're the leader? When your team succeeds, do you give the members of the team the credit? Rate yourself on a scale of 1 to 10. Where are you and why? Put a checkmark on the line. "1" represents the lowest and a "10" is the highest you can receive.

1   2   3   4   5   6   7   8   9   10

How often do you experience definite feelings of insecurity in your life and leadership? Circle one that most accurately communicates feelings of insecurity.

Each day   **Each week**   **Each year**

Check yourself each time you compare yourself to someone. Pause and thank God for the differences that He has given you.

Focus your attention on your strengths for a school semester or a season in your life. Identify and polish your gifts and skills during the rest of the school year. What are my strengths? How will you develop them?

Read and listen to motivational material: books, podcasts, magazines, websites, and so forth. What books, podcasts, magazines or websites will you invest in?

Identify the two or three most common lies you believe about yourself. Write down the truth about those areas in the space below, then tell yourself the truth.

Remind yourself of the truth: we are to imitate Christ—who came and emptied Himself in order to serve others, not to be served.

Never put your emotional health in the hands of someone else.

Build a network of support people who are "safe." Practice giving and receiving the love, encouragement, and truth you both need. Everyone needs a healthy network of people who replenish them and hold them accountable. Fill in the blanks of your network in the chart below.

MY NETWORK

Heroes
Those you look up to and admire
_____
_____

Models
Those who do what you want to do
_____
_____

Mentors
Those who coach you.
_____
_____

Inner Circle
Those who are closest to you
_____
_____

Followers
Those you invest in and lead.
_____
_____

BRINGING IT ALL HOME

French novelist Honoré de Balzac was a keen observer of human nature. He sought to capture a picture of modern civilization in his work "The Human Comedy." He once observed, "Nothing is a greater impediment to being on good terms with others than being ill at ease with yourself." Don't let insecurity prevent you from reaching your potential!

THE POWER OF PASSION

Finding Your Passion Will Increase Your
Level of Impact on the World

"As a deer longs for streams of water, so I long for You, God. I thirst for God, the living God. When can I come and appear before God?"
(Psalm 42:1-2).

Working with high school and college students over the years, I've thought many times: if I could give away just one trait to these next generation leaders, it would be passion.

Passion is the energy of our soul. It's the missing ingredient in most people's lives. I believe it's what enables an ordinary person to be extraordinary.

One of my favorite stories from NCAA football comes from the career of Bear Bryant, legendary coach of the Alabama Crimson Tide. (I'm not sure if this one is true or just an urban legend!) In the final minutes of a game Alabama had the ball and led by just a few points. All they had to do was hold on to the ball and victory was theirs.

Recognizing the opposition was expecting Alabama to play it safe, Bryant's quarterback talked his team into doing a pass play, and scoring again. It was very risky because if he threw an interception and the other team scored, Alabama would lose the game. The entire team hesitated in the huddle, but their quarterback persuaded them to do it. As he launched his pass downfield his worst nightmare was realized. He threw it right into the hands of the safety—the fastest player on the other team. In a flash he was off and running toward his own end zone. The entire Alabama team was after him, but he was just too fast. No one could keep up…until out of nowhere, Alabama's quarterback was gaining on him. At about the three-yard line the quarterback caught him and threw him to the ground, saving the game for Alabama. The last seconds of the clock ticked off and the Crimson Tide went on to win the game.

A man's destiny is not determined by what he possesses, but by what possesses him.

Afterward, Bear Bryant was approached by the opposing coach. "I want an explanation for what just happened out there," he said. "How did your quarterback outrun my fastest man?" Bear Bryant just smiled. "It's easy," he replied. "Your man was running for six points. My man was running for his life."

I chuckle at that story, but it illustrates an important truth. What motivates us has a lot to do with whether we reach our goal or not. If we don't have something to live and die for, we're not likely to work or play with passion. A man's destiny is not determined by what he possesses, but by what possesses him.

Passionate leaders have answered three important questions in their life:

1. What do you really want? *(This is about our desire)*

2. Why do you want it? *(This is about our motives)*

3. How badly do you want it? *(This is about our passion)*

WHAT IS PASSION?

Passion can be defined as an intense emotion that compels action. It's a strong devotion to some person, object, activity or concept. In this chapter, we'll cover two issues:
1. Living with passion.
2. Finding your passion.

People who've deeply influenced their world did so with passion; they had a narrow, all-consuming passion for a cause. In fact, passion was more important that their intellect. Over 50% of all CEO's of Fortune 500 companies had C or C- averages in school. 65% of all U.S. senators come from the bottom half of their school classes. 75% of U.S. presidents were in the lower half of their classes of school. Over 50% of millionaire entrepreneurs never finished college! So, how did they do it? One word: passion. While researching over five hundred top performers from all areas of work, the arts, and sports, Robert Kriegel made this statement: "No two were alike, but the one quality they had in common was passion. It was their drive, their enthusiasm, their desire that distinguished them."

This is true of countless influential men and women in history. They decided the key was simply to pursue their passion and leave the rest to God. Usually these men and women had a very narrow mission. They knew that leaders can do anything, but they can't do everything. Once they narrowed their focus, they blessed the world around them with their gift and their passion.

- David Brainard caught a vision to work with Native Americans. He cared so deeply for them he'd go out in the snow and pray, positioning himself on a hill that overlooked the reservations. He prayed so intensely for them the snow melted around him three feet in diameter. He prayed so long and intensely at his home, he wore grooves in the hard wood floors where his knees were daily.

- Dwight Moody preached to an audience in Chicago on the night of the great Chicago fire. He told them to come back the next night to make a decision for Christ. Many people who attended that night died in the fire. Moody was devastated. He determined he would never preach again without giving an opportunity for people to meet Christ. He also made a decision to win someone to Christ everyday for the rest of his life. He met people and shared every day until someone came to Christ. He wouldn't let himself sleep until they did.

- John Wesley preached an average of three sermons a day for 54 years. He so impacted England, four out of five pubs closed down in many villages and towns. Thousands stopped drinking because they had given their lives to Christ. When someone asked him why so many stopped to hear him speak, he responded, "I just light myself with the Spirit of God, and people come to watch me burn."

- Joan of Arc knew her life purpose by the time she was 15. When she was 17 she was leading 3,000 French knights in battle. At one point they came to a wall. She turned to an officer and said, "I will lead the way over the wall." The officer responded, "Not a man will follow you." Without hesitation she replied, "I won't be looking back to see if they are following."

PRINCIPLES ON PASSION

1. When you are passionate about something, commitment comes with the territory.
2. Passion turns your "have-to's" into "want-to's."
3. A passionate person with few resources will outgrow a passive one with many.
4. With passion, you'll enjoy the climb as much as reaching the summit.
5. A passionate person doesn't have to push himself to start; he has to force himself to stop.

PASSION IS RARE

What do the people in the previous stories have in common? Passion. So why is this so uncommon? Why doesn't everyone find their passion and pursue it? Why don't people live with passion each day? Let me suggest a few reasons why so few people have passion.

1. **They have allowed something precious to become common and familiar.** It is true. People, beliefs or causes that were once sources of passion become familiar. The novelty wears off and the passion leaks. We forget the stuff we really believe in.

2. **They want acceptance and approval.** Passion draws and repels people at the same time. Most people want to be accepted by the culture and fit in rather than stand out. They don't want to risk repelling anyone.

3. **Our society is passive.** We live in a culture that pushes for tolerance and political correctness. The unspoken pressure is not to stand for something; just sit still and watch YouTube videos or listen to music.

4. **Apathy tends to increase with age.** The longer you live the tougher it is to live with passion. We get jaded over time. Wise, balanced young leaders are rare…but so are zealous older believers.

5. **They have no purpose beyond themselves.** People who live for themselves are in a very small business. But that's how most people live. Their whole life revolves around "me, myself and I."

Passion draws and repels people at the same time.

REFLECT AND RESPOND

Has your passion leaked? Check those that apply generally to your life right now.

○ Yes   ○ Most of the time   ○ Not sure   ○ Just a little   ○ No

In your life, what causes your passion to leak? Jot down two or three items.

1.
2.
3.

What are you passionate about right now? Can you jot down a passion or some thoughts related to things you are passionate about? Use the space below.

WHAT DID JESUS SAY?

Let's take a look at the Book. In Matthew 13:44-46, Jesus told two stories about the Kingdom of God. In these parables Jesus shares the right perspective on God's kingdom and how we should approach this kingdom with our lives. "The kingdom of heaven is like a treasure hidden in a field, which a man found and hid; and from joy over it, he goes and sells all he has and buys the field. Again, the kingdom of heaven is like a merchant seeking fine pearls, and upon finding one pearl of great value, he went and sold all that he had, and bought it."

It is interesting to me that Jesus Christ makes some assumptions about us and about the kingdom of heaven. Think about it. Both the man and the merchant in the parables sold all they had in order to get the field and the pearl. Wow. Jesus seems to be saying that passion is the only appropriate way to approach His kingdom.

JESUS' ASSUMPTIONS ABOUT US AND ABOUT THE KINGDOM ARE CLEAR:

1. We perceive its value as greater than all other possessions.

2. We will give up personal possessions in order to obtain it.

3. We believe no sacrifice is too great to secure it for ourselves.

4. We want it more passionately than anything else in life.

These assumptions are right, but so distant from where most followers of Christ live today, at least in the North America. We SAY we love Jesus and His Kingdom more than anything else in our worship songs—but if someone were to watch our lives they would see a difference between what we sing and the way we live our lives daily. Is this true on your campus?

When it comes right down to it, we don't want to live with radical passion as Jesus assumed we would. The problem isn't that we don't have any passion at all. It's that we have many passions. God is just one of several passions we possess that make us feel inspired and secure. We certainly want God on our side as we venture out into our first job interview or when we plan our wedding, or buy a car, or so forth. Sometimes, we treat God like a good luck charm. We want Him around in case we get in trouble.

You may remember the story of Princess Diana and Prince Charles. When they first married it was called "The Wedding of the Century." Millions watched on TV around the world. It was so elegant. So romantic.

Unfortunately, all the passion was lost. The wedding became a marriage run by protocol and routines. By 1990, they were only civil with each other. They posed for photographs, but it was clear the passion was gone. They were cordial and shared their sons' lives. Soon, they separated and eventually, they were divorced. Such a sad story that ended with her tragic death.

I wonder sometimes if this might be a good analogy for many of us. When we first come to Christ there is often great passion. We even use the term

Jesus seems to be saying that passion is the only appropriate way to approach His kingdom.

"on fire for God." We're hot. Eventually, however, we lose it. Like a slow leak in your car tire, we don't even notice we've lost the bounce and the energy we once had. We call it "maturity." But really it's a loss of our childlike faith that Jesus said we need to enter the Kingdom of heaven (Matthew 18:3). It isn't that we're against God. We still do the routines. We "shake His hand" on Sunday by mouthing some song lyrics. But there is no passion. It's like a stale marriage. We have full heads and busy hands, but an empty heart.

REFLECT AND RESPOND

List the top five things you are passionate about in your life. Be honest. Where does God's kingdom fit into that list? Is He even on the top-five? Where does He rank?

1.
2.
3.
4.
5.

Share with your accountability partner why you are passionate about your top-five list. The space below is for you to jot down some thoughts before you share with others.

LESSONS FROM THE PARABLES

Let's unpack the truths we learn from the parables Jesus told in Matthew 13:44-46.

1. The Kingdom of God must be personally appropriated.

It's a fact - people don't just wander into the Kingdom of God. The term "Kingdom of God" means the rule and reign of God. It means surrender. Passion comes from total surrender. It causes us to give our time, our money and our talents for something. That's why apathy is its opposite. The word "apathy" is taken from two roots: "a" which means without; and "pathos" which means passion. We don't get passionate about God's Kingdom just hanging around or by having "tenure" in the Body of Christ. Time doesn't guarantee it. It is not automatic. You must personally go after it.

Group Up

How have you developed your passion over time?

2. The Kingdom of God is priceless.

The pearl in the parable could be likened to a diamond today. The merchant gave up the prospects of all the other pearls he owned or might find in order to get this one pearl of great value. In other words, he removed all his other options.

Think about how the conversation might go if you or I spotted this valuable pearl. I wonder if the negotiation might go something like this:

"I want this pearl. How much is it?"
"Well," the seller says, "it is very expensive."
"But, how much?" I ask.
'Well, a very large amount."
"Do you think I could buy it?"
"Oh, of course. Everyone can buy it."
"But didn't you say it was very expensive?"
"Yes."
"Well how much is it?"
"Everything you have," says the seller.
I make up my mind, "All right, I'll buy it."
"Well, what do you have?" the seller wants to know. "Let's write it down."
"Well, I have ten thousand dollars in the bank."
"Good—ten thousand dollars. What else?"
"That's all. That's all I have."
"Nothing more?"
"Well, I have a few dollars here in my pocket."
"How much?"
I start digging. "Well, let's see—fifteen, twenty, thirty, forty, sixty dollars."
"That's fine. What else do you have?"
"Well nothing. That's all."
"Where do you live?" He's still probing.
"In my house. Yes, I have a house."
"The house, too, then." He writes that down.
"You mean I have to live in my camper?"
"Oh, you have a camper? That too. What else?"
"I'll have to sleep in my car."
"You have a car?"
"Two of them."

"Both become mine, both cars. What else?"

"Well, you already have my money, my house, my camper, my cars. What more do you want from me?"

"Are you alone in this world?"

"No, I have a wife and two children."

"Oh, really. Yes, your wife and two children will be part of the deal, too. What else?"

"I have nothing left! I, alone, am left now!"

Suddenly the seller exclaims, "Of course, you are included too. Everything becomes mine—wife, children, house, money, cars and you."

Then he goes on. "Now listen—I will allow you to use all of these things for the time being, but don't forget that everything is mine, as well as you. And remember, whenever I need any of them you must give them up because now I am the owner."

3. The kingdom of God is the source of true joy.

Did you notice in the parables that both men—the man who bought the field and the merchant who bought the pearl—did it out of joy. No one had to talk them into it; or coerce them into some religious activity out of duty or obligation. Joy was the motive, not rules or regulations. This reminds me that we were created to experience the kingdom of God in our lives. That's why Jesus assumes we'll be passionate about entering it.

I once heard a story about a fish that wondered what life would be like above the water. He could see folks up there on the land and began thinking that maybe he was missing out on something. "I am all cooped up underwater while humans have all the fun," he muttered to himself. So, he decided he'd soar to the surface of the water and flop out onto the dry land. After trying several times he finally succeeded.

At first it felt different but good. There was warm sunshine on the beach and a cool breeze. He saw colors everywhere. It was great. Eventually, however, he started struggling to breathe. He felt like he was suffocating. He began to flop around trying to get some comfort. As he did so, a rabbit hopped over and saw his dilemma. He spoke up. "I see your problem, Mr. Fish. You need a martini. You are just too stressed out right now. A good drink will fix you up." The rabbit poured a martini on the fish. At first, it felt good—kind of like being underwater. But eventually he was fighting to breathe again.

People don't just wander into the kingdom of God.

Group Up
What causes you to lose your passion?

After a few minutes a squirrel happened by. "I see what your problem is," he said. "You just need to get some nuts to eat. That always makes me feel better." So the squirrel ran and got some nuts and poured them all over the fish. Again, the fish felt good for a while. It felt right to be submerged under something. But soon, he felt out of place again.

One animal after another approached the fish and diagnosed his problem. Each one failed to provide a lasting solution for the fish. After several hours the fish became desperate. He began flopping around wildly…until by accident, he flopped into the water. Ahhhh, he thought. This is where I belong. I am finally home.

People try so many things to satisfy their longings. We muster a passion for sports, boyfriends, courses, parties, scholarships and careers. Those are all fine, but they were never designed to fill the need for long-term fulfillment. We listen to bogus advice from people who mean well, but don't understand how humans are wired. We're created to live with passion for something deeper…the kingdom of God.

We were created to experience the Kingdom of God in our lives.

4. The Kingdom of God must be sought after with great intensity.
Jesus made this statement in Matthew 11:12, "From the days of John the Baptist until now, the kingdom of heaven has been suffering violence, and violent men have been seizing it by force."

Bible scholars differ as to exactly what Jesus meant by this statement. One truth is for certain; God's kingdom isn't something you experience accidentally. You must pursue it. It isn't some cerebral decision you make in your head. The kingdom life isn't a life you can live passively. There is no room for apathy; it requires passion. The only appropriate way to enter the kingdom of God is with passion.

Passion is what causes people to excel.

Passion is that little extra that makes all the difference between an ordinary person and an extraordinary one; between a casual Christian and an influential one. It's like the part of your blanket that hangs over the edge of the bed. It is only a little bit more blanket, but it is that part that keeps you warm at night. It's the little extra. At 211 degrees, water is hot enough to shave with or heat some soup on the stove. At 212 degrees, it becomes steam, powerful enough to move a locomotive along a railroad track. That's just one degree but it makes a big difference. That's how passion works. Passion will make up for what you lack in resources. Great things have been achieved by those who didn't have big budgets, or big talent, or a big team of people—they just had lots of passion.

As far as I'm concerned, Pete Gray deserves to be in Baseball's Hall of Fame. I say this because Pete Gray had a dream when he was growing up. He wanted to play major league baseball and he wanted to play at least one game in Yankee stadium. Amazingly, Pete reached both of those goals, but that's not why I think he should be in the Hall of Fame. What is astounding is that he reached both of those goals despite the fact that he had only one arm! (Not just one hand—but one arm!) Can you imagine hitting major league pitching with just one arm? Or, fielding major league hits and throwing runners out with just one arm? His manager once said, "Pete Gray is not handicapped. We are the ones that are handicapped. It takes us two arms to do what he does with one."

I have a question for you. What made up for Pete Gray's lack of an arm? I believe it was passion. His passion made up for what he lacked in resources.

Passion is what causes people to excel. It pushes them past logic and reason to perform in an excellent way. It doesn't always go against logic; it just takes us beyond logic. For instance, I remember reading a newspaper article about a young man who had been badly burned in a house fire. He was asleep when the basement furnace caught on fire. Before the firefighters could get him out, he'd suffered first, second and third degree burns on his body. When he awoke in the intensive care unit, the first request he had was for someone to bring him his Bible. When he got it, he was depressed to find that he couldn't see well enough to read the words of Scripture. Someone even brought him a large print Bible—but it still didn't help. Later, he requested the Bible on CDs so he could listen to God's Word. Sadly, when they arrived he discovered his hearing was so bad he couldn't even make out the words on the recording. Finally, he asked for a Bible written in Braille, for the blind. He felt this was his last chance to soak in God's Word with his physical condition. But, alas, when it arrived, he pressed his fingers against the raised letters of the Bible only to find he had lost so much of the feeling in his fingers that he could not even make out the print. He began to weep. He was devastated. But as he grieved over his loss he happened to put the Bible up

Group Up
Discuss the time in your life when you were most passionate about God's kingdom.

What has happened since then?

to his lips to kiss it. By accident his tongue happened to touch the Braille letters. He could feel them! His tongue was able to distinguish the shapes of the letters. Once again he had hope. At the time this article was written, the young man had read through the entire New Testament twice... with his tongue!

REFLECT AND RESPOND

Share with your accountability partner, if you have one, how your life stacks up to the four lessons from Jesus' parables.

1.
2.
3.
4.

Which lesson is most difficult for you to live out in your life?

HUNGRY, ANYONE?

Many times God had to get his people to a "hungry" place; a place where they were desperate for Him or for the vision He had given them. We rarely accomplish big goals unless we have hungry hearts. God had to prepare Moses in the wilderness for forty years until he was focused; God had to break Jacob for years, until he was ready to wrestle with God all night for His blessing. In my own life, God had to get me past my search for pleasures, sports, girlfriends, and grades—even though none of those are evil in themselves. They simply displaced God and His vision for me, and diluted my passion. I remember breaking up with a Christian girlfriend because we were distracting each other from the pursuit of God. It was messy and difficult, but well worth it. I felt like a weight had been taken off my shoulders afterward, because I was free to pursue my calling.

In my freshman year of college I dove into ministry opportunities. I loved serving people and sharing Christ and seeing lives change. That year, a senior named Dan approached me and asked if we could talk. I was not prepared for what he said.

Dan had been watching my passion for God and interpreted it as immaturity. He was studying to go into the ministry, and as a senior he'd become jaded by his theology courses. He saw me as an inexperienced freshman who was trying to make a big splash for himself. He insulted me and told me I needed to grow up. Regarding my passion and enthusiasm, he said I would "get over it." I was just young and immature.

I walked out of his dorm room a little devastated. When I returned to my room I knelt down and prayed. In my prayer time I sorted through my motives. I determined that it was not immaturity that made me pursue the things I did. I was in love with God and the calling He had given me. I resolved that I would not lose my passion. That little meeting with Dan turned out to be a blessing for me. It sparked me to commit myself to a life of passion, even as I grew older and more experienced.

Ironically, Dan stayed around the campus for the next three years doing graduate work. During my senior year Dan saw me in the media center, and stopped me. We had not talked for years. This time he sought my forgiveness. He apologized for what he said. He told me he'd continued to watch me and realized now that this wasn't a show. I was for real and my passion was genuine. He even thanked me for the example I set.

As my wife will attest I am far from perfect, I share that little story for one simple reason. Passion is often seen as a trait for immature people. Seasoned veterans become polished and sophisticated…but not passionate. This is wrong. You must commit to hold fast to the passion you possess during your younger years. Don't let anyone rob you of it.

REFLECT AND RESPOND

Are you hungry for God? Are you hungry to pursue your God-given calling? Check the box that applies to your life at present.

○ *Yes, always*
○ *Most of the time*
○ *Usually*
○ *Some of the time*
○ *Not so far*

Are there people in your life that steal your passion? What can you do about it?

We rarely accomplish big goals unless we have hungry hearts.

Your intimacy with God directly impacts your passion for God and for life.

LIVING WITH PASSION

So, what can we do to both find our passion and live with passion? Good questions. Let's begin with some basic principles we must embrace.

1. Believe that passion is the deciding difference in your life.
Soren Kierkegaard warned of the danger of the church losing her passion for the gospel, treating it like a piece of information. He compared it to reading a cookbook to a person who is hungry. Passion is the fire that ignites action. We must have it. Titus 2:14 reminds us that "God gave Himself for us to redeem us…and purify for Himself a people that are His very own, eager for what is good." The literal Greek meaning for the word "eager" is zealous or passionate.

2. Take personal responsibility to become intimate with God.
We discussed this in an earlier chapter. Your intimacy with God directly impacts your passion for God and for life. Intimate Christians don't have to fake passion; it isn't plastic or artificial. What's more, when you're intimate with God your fire will burn even when you are doing the small things in life.

3. Invest time digging for pearls.
Jesus spoke of the merchant finding the pearl of great value. We must spend time in God's Word digging for pearls of insight that will ignite a flame for obedience. However, it won't happen unless we invest time and energy digging. We must be intentional.

4. Associate with people of passion.
Remember the analogy of the hot coals. When they are together—they stay hot. When you separate one from the rest, it cools down. One of the best ways to stay passionate is to hang out with others who are passionate. Remember what King Solomon wrote: "He who walks with the wise becomes wise" (Proverbs 13:20).

5. Identify your personal passion.
While I hope you maintain a passion for Jesus Christ, you will want to identify a personal passion for your life. It will start with simple interests. Then, you will notice a burden for a certain need. Later, it will preoccupy your attention. Finally, you will want to act on it. It will consume you. I suggest you look over the list you made in chapter one, when you exam-

Group Up
What enables you to become passionate?
What helps you maintain your passion?

ined your life mission. If you have not yet done so, take the assessment called: My Passion Profile. Go to: www.MyPassionProfile.com to take it and clarify what your deepest passions are. Your passion will fuel your mission. Tim Redmond wrote: "There are many things that will catch my eye, but there are only a few things that will catch my heart…it is those I consider to pursue."

6. Remember what God has done for you.
This is critical. We lose passion when we forget what God has done in the past. This is why He constantly had His people celebrate and remember His miracles and blessings as they wandered through the wilderness. Take time to count your blessings and reflect on the goodness of God.

7. Avoid things that dull your spiritual hunger.
My guess is, you know the things that cause you to become lethargic or apathetic toward God and your purpose in life. You must decide to avoid those things before you get into a situation and you cannot do anything about it.

8. Ask God to build a hungry heart in you.
This may be the best step of all. You might have to pray, "Lord, make me willing to be willing." Ask God to give you a passion for Him, for life and to help you find your passion in life. He said He will give liberally to those who ask.

HOW BADLY DO YOU WANT IT?
There is an old story about the Greek philosopher, Socrates. He was sitting beside a lake when a young man approached him and asked him how he could get the wisdom that Socrates had. He told the wise philosopher he would do anything to get it.

With that, Socrates motioned for the young man to follow him as he walked into the lake. He got deeper and deeper until both of them were waist high in water. At that point Socrates asked the young man, "What did you say you wanted?"

The young man replied, "I want wisdom." With that, Socrates put his hand on the man's head and shoved it under the water. He held it there for several seconds before he let go. When the young man surfaced he

> "There are many things that will catch my eye, but there are only a few things that will catch my heart."

had a bewildered look on his face. He didn't know what Socrates was up to. But before he could ask Socrates asked him the question again. The young man hesitated, but answered, "Wisdom."

Again, Socrates shoved the young man's head under the water. This time he held it under longer. Finally, the young man thrust his head upward only to find Socrates asking the same question. For the third time, the young man responded that he wanted wisdom.

This time, Socrates shoved his head under water and held it there for a long period of time. In fact, he held it there until the young man could take it no longer. He thrust his head up and gasped for air. Immediately, Socrates asked: "What is it you want?"

This time the young man was honest. He screamed, "Air! I want air!"

With that, Socrates just smiled and said, "Well then. When you want wisdom the way you wanted air just a second ago, you will get it."

My sentiments exactly. When you want God—when you want anything in life—the way you want the air you breathe, you will get it. Passion is the key.

"When you want wisdom the way you wanted air just a second ago, you will get it."

ASSESSMENT

What is your number one passion today?

On a scale of 1 to 10, with 10 being the highest, how passionate would you rate your relationship with Jesus Christ today? Put a mark on the line to indicate where you would be.

1   2   3   4   5   6   7   8   9   10

How can you increase your passion for Jesus Christ?

APPLICATION

Interview a person who you see as a passionate person. Ask him what he's done to build his passion over time. Choose to do one item he shares in order to increase your own passion for a life in Jesus Christ.

THAT'S A WRAP!

This wraps up, Exploring Your Identity Sharpening Your Focus. If you have not experienced the other elements in the "Flourish" package, you can find them at: *www.GrowingLeaders.com.*

This resource is created for you to help you develop Christian leadership during your high school and college years. I trust that once you have gone through the workbook, you've found it relevant and helpful.

My prayer is that your life will be one of "salt and light" for your generation and the next. You will transform society for the kingdom of God,

For the entire "Flourish" package or for other resources to help you grow as a young leader, check out: www.GrowingLeaders.com.

Here's to your best days ahead.